Also from t[illegible]

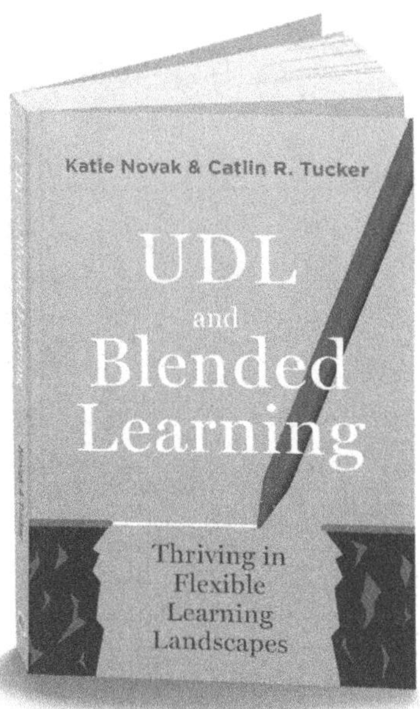

You can develop the skills to meet the needs of learners in any learning environment.

This approachable, in-depth guide unites the adaptability of Universal Design for Learning with the flexibility of blended learning, equipping educators with the tools they need to create relevant, authentic, and meaningful learning pathways to meet students where they're at, no matter the time and place or their pace and path. With step-by-step guidance and clear strategies, authors Katie Novak and Catlin Tucker empower teachers to implement these frameworks in the classroom, with a focus on cultivating community, building equity, and increasing accessibility for all learners.

As we face increasing uncertainty and frequent disruption to traditional ways of living and learning, *UDL and Blended Learning* offers bold, innovative, inclusive solutions for navigating a range of learning landscapes, from the home to the classroom and all points in between, no matter what obstacles may lie ahead.

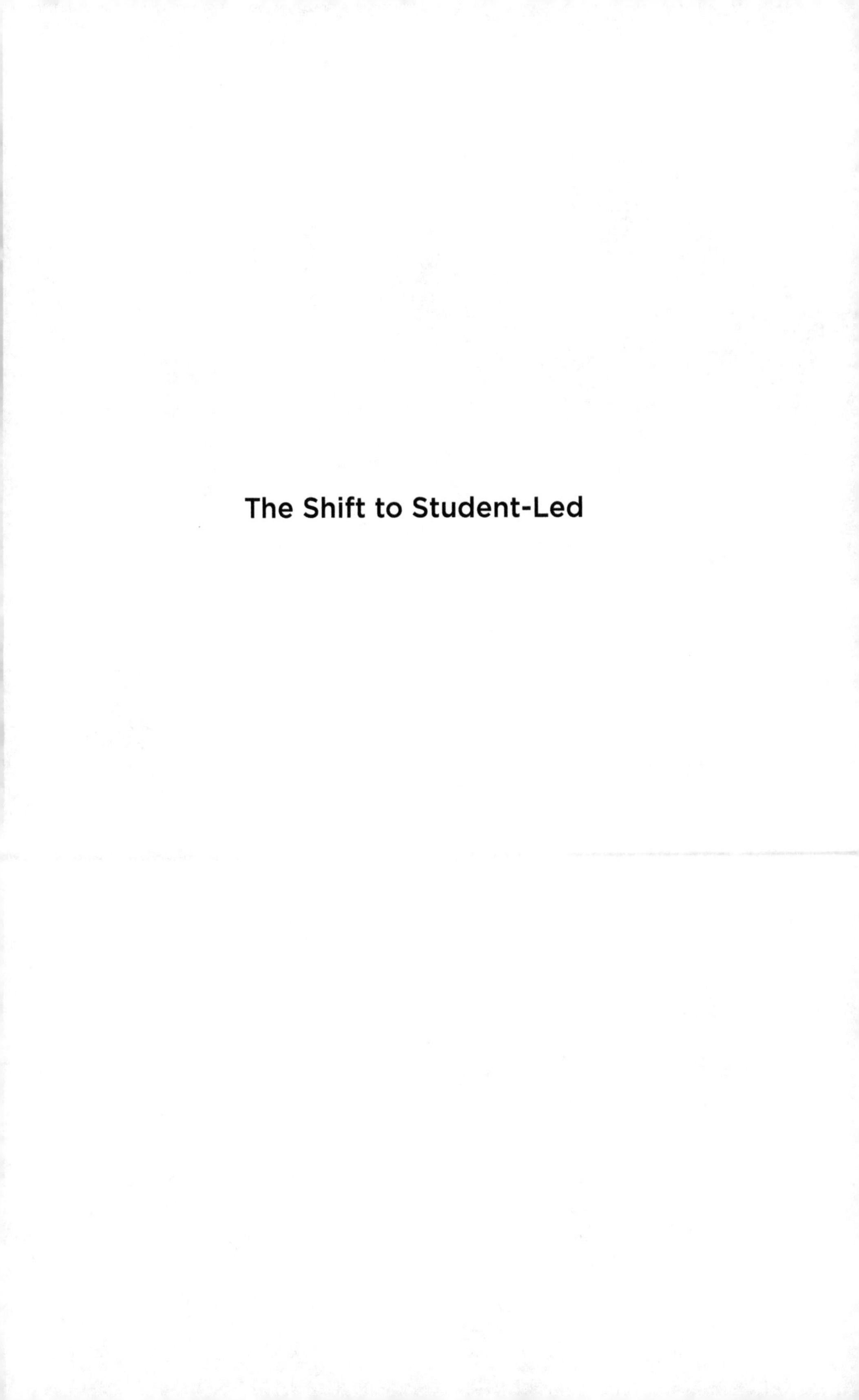

The Shift to Student-Led

Catlin R. Tucker & Katie Novak

The Shift to Student Led

Reimagining Classroom Workflows with UDL and Blended Learning

The Shift to Student-Led: Reimagining Classroom Workflows with UDL and Blended Learning

Published by IMPress, a division of Dave Burgess Consulting, Inc.
IMPressbooks.org
DaveBurgessConsulting.com
San Diego, CA

Library of Congress Control Number: 2022946632
Paperback ISBN: 978-1-948334-52-5
Ebook ISBN: 978-1-948334-53-2

Cover design by Emily Mahon
Interior design by Liz Schreiter
Edited and produced by Reading List Editorial
ReadingListEditorial.com

Cheyenne and Maddox, you are a daily reminder of how different two people can be, even when they've been raised in the same environment by the same parents! My hope for you and for every child is that your teachers will celebrate those differences and find ways to help each of you discover your strengths and pursue your passions!

As a daughter of two teachers, I was born for this. To Mom and Dad, thank you for your example, your passion, all your Newport Creamery sundae runs, and the whole raising me thing. I learned from the best. Love, Katie

Contents

Tables, Figures, and Planning Templates

To access templates and other resources mentioned in this book, use this QR code.

INTRODUCTION

The Why Driving This Book

Catlin As I get older and the pace of life speeds up, I've begun waking up earlier and earlier. The wee hours of the morning before my kids get up and the day begins are my most productive. I usually spend this time in bed with a cup of coffee working on presentations or preparing for a coaching session on my calendar that day.

The morning I realized I needed to write this book was different. I had three consecutive days off from speaking, facilitating training sessions, and coaching. I decided not to spend my morning working and instead started reading *Daring Greatly* by Brené Brown. Her words about the importance of courage, compassion, and connection struck me. It's uncanny how books find me just when I need them.

Professionally, I have struggled with the resistance to change in education even after the tumult of the pandemic rocked our lives in 2020. I hoped that one silver lining of the pandemic would be that educators and educational institutions would realize that the way we have approached this work in the past is not flexible or dynamic enough for an uncertain future. Traditional one-size-fits-all approaches to designing and facilitating lessons do not make learning accessible, inclusive, or equitable for *all* students. That is why Katie and I wrote *UDL and Blended Learning: Thriving in Flexible Learning Landscapes*.

Katie and I wanted to arm teachers with two complementary frameworks to help them develop a mindset, skill set, and tool set nimble enough to navigate any single teaching and learning landscape with confidence. Yet we've heard many teachers express a desire to return to the status quo as schools reopened. We worry about losing the gains and momentum from the last two years in favor of what is familiar and comfortable. Familiarity and comfort may work for some teachers, but we don't think it is best for students.

As with most things in my life, I read Brené Brown's book through the lens of an educator. Her emphasis on courage, compassion, and connection as essential to wholehearted living made me think about the shape these take in our work as educators.

- How can we be *more* courageous in this work?
- Where is compassion showing up in our treatment of ourselves and our students?
- How do we develop stronger connections with the people (i.e., colleagues and students) in our lives?

As I contemplated these questions, I kept thinking about how universally designed blended learning requires teachers to be courageous, have compassion for themselves and their students, and create more opportunities for connection. I want to help teachers be courageous, compassionate, and able to prioritize connections in their work.

I immediately texted Katie with my idea for this book. Her response was "Oh my word. Yes! I'm in. Teachers are drowning."

I share this moment of inspiration because, quite frankly, this book would not have come to fruition if I had not had the time and space to let my mind wander. Too often, I run from one thing to another without allowing my brain the creative space to consider, question, wonder, discover, imagine, or innovate. I am not alone in this. Life is complex and demanding. These stolen moments may feel like luxuries, but they are not. They are valuable and necessary to our creativity and continued professional growth.

Most educators lament not having enough time for all the work they feel they *should* be doing. They are bombarded by paper work, emails, meetings, and grading. These tasks extend into their lives beyond the classroom, invading their evenings and weekends. The problem is that when we are wading through endless paper work, emails, or grading, we don't have the mental energy or space to let our minds wander and engage in the creative aspects of this work, like designing dynamic learning experiences. I want teachers to have more time to spend reading, exercising, engaging with friends and family, and enjoying quiet moments that free their minds to take part in what I think of as intellectual play. It is in these moments that some of our best ideas for how to engage students will emerge.

I remember a night in 2014 when I was exhausted after a long day at work. Instead of doing the hundred other things I felt I *should* be doing, I decided to kick my feet up and watch Jimmy Fallon's *The Tonight Show*. Bryan Cranston was the guest, and he played a game with Jimmy Fallon called Word Sneak. Each man had a set of cards with random words on them. The goal of the game was to "sneak" those words into the conversation casually and seamlessly. Their conversation was hilarious. I giggled through the whole game! I immediately thought, "I want to do this with my students!" Word Sneak quickly became my students' favorite way to practice using their new vocabulary words. Yet the inspiration for that game never would have happened if I hadn't taken a break from work and watched that episode of *The Tonight Show*.

I've had countless other moments like this. Each time I get a burst of inspiration in a quiet moment, it is a reminder of how much more creative I am when I give myself a break.

Why

I hope this book accomplishes two goals. First, I want teachers to rediscover their joy and reengage in this profession. Second, I want students to develop into expert learners capable of sharing ownership of learning, so teachers are not doing the lion's share of the work.

The last few years in education have taken a toll on teachers. Many of the teachers Katie and I work with express frustration and disillusionment with this profession. They are drowning in work and unrealistic demands. Many teachers are also mentally and emotionally exhausted by the uncertainty created by the pandemic. They need concrete strategies they can use to reimagine their approach to this work so that it feels sustainable and rewarding.

Students also need to learn how to fully engage in the learning process. In many classrooms, students are still occupying the role of silent observer and consumer. They are not challenged to develop their metacognitive muscles, assess their work, provide each other with substantive feedback, and communicate their progress with the people in their lives. That translates into students who are not invested in their learning. Learning is something that is happening *to* them. They are much like fans sitting in the stands watching a game unfold on the field. Instead, students need to be active, engaged participants in the learning process. This is the only way to cultivate expert learners who are resourceful, strategic, motivated, and self-aware. The more students actively engage in all parts of the learning process, the less pressure there is on the teacher to do all of the work.

How

In this book, we focus on reimagining ten time-consuming teacher-led workflows in education. We focus on one traditional teacher-led workflow in each chapter and describe how to make it sustainable and student-led.

- Workflow Shift #1: From Transfer of Information to Student Discovery
- Workflow Shift #2: From Whole-Group Teacher-Led to Small-Group Student-Led Discussion
- Workflow Shift #3: From Reading as Solitary Endeavor to Reading for Connection
- Workflow Shift #4: From an Audience of One to an Authentic Audience
- Workflow Shift #5: From Teacher-Created to Student-Generated Review and Practice
- Workflow Shift #6: From Formative Assessment as Teacher Tool to a Metacognitive Tool for Learners
- Workflow Shift #7: From Feedback on Finished Products to Feedback during the Process
- Workflow Shift #8: From Teacher Assessment to Self-Assessment
- Workflow Shift #9: From Teachers Initiating Parent Communication to Learners Owning the Conversation about Their Progress
- Workflow Shift #10: From Teacher Project Design to Student-Led Project-Based Learning

Each chapter will follow a similar format: First, we unpack the problems with the "old way" of doing things and identify the aspects of these approaches that are unsustainable. We call this section "Research and Reality." Then we offer specific strategies for reimagining the workflow from a student-led perspective. These strategies are designed to be flexible enough to work in any teaching and learning landscape—in a classroom, online, or a blend of the two.

We will anchor these student-led workflows in blended learning and UDL to highlight how universally designed blended learning creates the time and space for these shifts in your work with students. Shifting workflows isn't realistic in a teacher-centered, whole-group, lockstep environment. They require that teachers give students more control over their learning experience. Teachers must leverage blended learning models to partner with students and shift them to the center of the learning process for these shifts to be successful.

In addition, we make clear connections to the core beliefs at the heart of UDL to ensure that these strategies are accessible, inclusive, and equitable. We describe how these shifts can help you to align your practices with the core beliefs: a) that learner variability is the norm, b) all students are capable of working toward firm goals but need flexible means, and c) cultivating expert learners is critical if students are going to fully engage in the learning process.

Each chapter ends with a wrap-up that presents the big takeaways and includes a set of reflection and discussion questions for you, your book study group, or your professional learning community (PLC) to consider and discuss as you read. Finally, we have added an action item to the end of each chapter. This activity is designed to get you *acting* on what you are learning. It will challenge you to take what you learned in the chapter and create something you can implement immediately.

The workflows we describe in this book are fundamental shifts in the way we think about our role and the role of students in the learning process. You may worry that students are not capable of sharing the responsibility of learning; however, that fear is an indication that students need *more*, not fewer, opportunities to fully engage in the learning process. Katie and I hope that you will share what you are learning with a wider community on your campus and online as you read, learn, experiment, and refine your practice. We want this book to spark more conversations about how universally designed blended learning can help teachers create more sustainable approaches to this work.

You may worry that students are not capable of sharing the responsibility of learning; however, that fear is an indication that students need more, not fewer, opportunities to fully engage in the learning process.

What

Katie and I would love for every teacher who reads this book to find a more sustainable and balanced approach to this work. We want teachers to have time to relax and recharge on their evenings and weekends. We do not want teachers to sacrifice precious time with family, friends, or themselves because they are dealing with a never-ending to-do list. We hope that teachers will have the mental space to get inspired in the time recovered by reimagining these traditional workflows. Just as I've been inspired by random moments in my life—the way a game of "would you rather" on a road trip with my kids led to a simple strategy I use to onboard teachers designing lessons that include student agency—I want other teachers to have more of those magical moments.

This reimagining requires courage, compassion, and connection. We must have the courage to question the status quo, face our fears, and take professional risks to find better ways of approaching this work.

We must be compassionate with ourselves and our students. These shifts will take time and practice. We must approach this work as the "lead learner" and be gentle with ourselves as we experiment, reflect, and improve. We also need to remember that these shifts will be new for our students and cause them to stretch. This may feel uncomfortable at first, because you are asking students to assume more cognitive and social responsibility for their learning. They will need clear routines, support, and skill building to feel confident leading the learning in these reimagined workflows.

Finally, this work requires connection with our colleagues and our students. Learning is, in part, a social endeavor. We will be more successful shifting fundamental approaches to our work if we are connected to a community of learners and co-create an environment that distributes the cognitive load and allows students to build agency and ownership in expert learning.

DYNAMIC DUO

UDL and Blended Learning

Universally Designed Spa Day

Katie

Every year, when my husband, Lon, asks me what I want for my birthday, I immediately respond, "The same as every year," which is code for "spa day." I love everything about the spa: the quiet, the smell of jasmine, the hot pillows they put on your neck in the waiting room, and the menu of services. There is something for everyone! If you're in for a quick trip, you can grab a thirty-minute minifacial. Just want to soak in the hot tub and lounge in a room that smells like eucalyptus and has the sound of crashing waves piped in? You got it! Want your partner to pull out all the stops and get you a massage and a facial for your birthday? (Yes, please!)

But here's the thing: Not all spas are created equal.

One birthday, Lon booked me a facial at a new day spa. Everything started as planned. I sipped a cup of chamomile tea in the waiting room, wrapped myself in a warm robe, and then cozied onto a heated table. A lovely woman came in quietly and introduced herself. She asked me if the heat of the table was okay. She asked me if I was allergic to anything. She asked what I did for work. She asked me if I had a dog when I was seven. Okay, that was an exaggeration, but she kept asking questions, not only before she gave me the facial but during the facial. At one point I nodded off, and when I woke up, she was still talking. She was absolutely lovely, and in a coffee shop, I would have loved to get to know her. But that was not how I pictured my spa day. Now, I know that many of you would *love* to chat with your aesthetician. When I get my hair done, I talk the entire time with my stylist, but when I'm at the spa, I want it to be quiet.

The facial was amazing, but that is a place I wouldn't go back to, because the experience wasn't for me. I didn't think much about that facial until this fall when I resumed my birthday spa day ritual. As I filled out the online forms, I stopped and silently celebrated. On the questionnaire, among the COVID screening questions and general questions about medical history and allergies, I had to answer questions like:

- If we use any oils for massage, which of the following scents do you prefer?
- What pressure would you like for your massage experience?

And the masterstroke:

- How much talking do you prefer to do with your technician?

    A) I like to talk during treatments.
    B) I like a little conversation initially and then prefer quiet.
    C) I prefer silence unless there are questions about the treatment.

As much as I love to talk in almost every setting, I chose B. I would love a minute or two to get to know the person examining my pores, but then I can settle in and snuggle up.

This story exemplifies the power of the Universal Design for Learning (UDL) framework. UDL approaches planning using three core beliefs: a) embracing variability, b) articulating firm goals, and c) fostering expert learning.

Variability is the understanding that no two people are the same, and no one person is the same all the time. All of us have different strengths, interests, and areas where we need to grow, and depending on the context, what we need is constantly changing. This variability is expected and should be anticipated when designing learning experiences. Essentially, we need our learners to reflect on their options and ask themselves, "What do I need *right now* to reach a goal?"

If you know me well, you know I'm a talker. I LOVE to chat and get to know people. I am excited about having conversations and getting to know people in most settings. But when I'm at the spa, I prefer quiet. Spa-vibe Katie is different from Katie in most other settings. That is because when the context changes, my needs change. And someday, I may visit a spa and feel an incredible urge to connect with someone. In that instance, I may choose the option "I like to talk during treatments."

The Power of Universal Design for Learning

As individuals, we are incredibly dynamic, and one-size-fits-all experiences don't often meet our needs. As you're reading this, you may be thinking, "Yeah, yeah, I get what you're saying with the spa, but sometimes in life, you don't get to choose. I mean, no one gives me a choice about whether to file my taxes." Well, technically, you have many choices when you file your taxes. Bear with us.

UDL practitioners talk about "firm goals, flexible means" as a way of recognizing shared outcomes and the numerous paths that can be used to get to them. At the spa, the goal is for everyone to have a relaxing experience. For some, that means having a conversation. For others, it means enjoying silence. When it comes to taxes, some people will print out the tax forms and file them through the mail. Others will e-file, use TurboTax, or hire an accountant.

When you design learning experiences with UDL, ask yourself, "What is it that all learners need to know or be able to do?" And then from there, consider, based on variability, "What are some options and choices to get there?" Approaching planning through the lens of UDL requires us to design an environment where students can choose their pathway, product, and pace as they work toward firm goals.

In more traditional models, teachers were the ones making decisions for learners. Instead, we need to encourage students to become expert learners, which means they reflect on firm goals and then consider their strengths, interests, mood, areas of need, etc. When we provide opportunities for learners to be more self-aware, they learn to examine multiple pathways and choose the ones that best meet their needs at the moment. Allowing students to choose what they need when they need it incorporates UDL, social-emotional learning, and trauma-informed and culturally sustaining practices. When we position students to drive their learning experience, we help students become expert learners who are self-aware, recognize the purpose of learning, and can make responsible, strategic decisions about their education.

When we provide opportunities for learners to be more self-aware, they learn to examine multiple pathways and choose the ones that best meet their needs at the moment. Allowing students to choose what they need when they need it incorporates UDL, social-emotional learning, and trauma-informed and culturally sustaining practices.

With UDL, teachers transition to the role of facilitator, removing barriers to learning by giving students options and choices to reach firm goals or rigorous state standards. To universally design lessons, teachers must design instruction with the three UDL principles: a) multiple means of engagement, b) multiple means of representation, and c) multiple means of action and expression.

When teachers provide multiple means of engagement, they are clear about firm goals and provide students with flexible means. Engagement extends beyond recruiting interest and providing choice. We also have to ensure that students can commit to the learning process and continue to put in effort and persistence when learning is challenging, they are exhausted, or they aren't super interested in the firm goals.

We must create classrooms where students feel safe enough to take risks and know they have options to cope. Creating practices and procedures that embrace frequent breaks, embedded scaffolds, revisions, and retakes can optimize student motivation. Since we are asking students to personalize their learning, it is important that we offer frequent opportunities for them to get feedback from peers and adults, reflect on their decisions, and course-correct, if necessary.

Representation is the process of collecting and presenting information to learners. For the last two hundred years of education, the primary means of representation have been text and talking (i.e., reading books and the whole-class lecture). Text is a problem for some people. Obviously, if you have a visual impairment, printed text creates a significant barrier. But it is also a problem for those who are English language learners or struggle with decoding, reading comprehension, dyslexia, or ADHD. Talking or lecturing is also a problem, as it requires hearing and strong auditory processing. Additionally, lecturing is often a passive activity that fails to engage the learner in the process.

As the founders of UDL state in *Universal Design For Learning: Theory and Practice*, "No single medium works for every learner, nor does it for every subject. . . . To promote understanding of information, concepts, relationships, and ideas, it is critical to provide multiple ways for learners to approach them."[1] When teachers provide multiple means of representation, learners get to make choices about how they learn, build knowledge, and explore resources as they work toward firm goals.

Imagine you attend a faculty meeting where the goal is that all educators will share best practices in lesson design. To activate background knowledge, there are printed packets of a peer-reviewed article about coherent lesson design. The task is simple. You will have twenty minutes to read the article in silence, and then you will join small groups to make connections between the article and your own practice. What fun!

Both of us have experienced meetings like this. Here's the thing: We are 100 percent certain that a single article will not meet the needs of all educators. In every school, there are nurses, school psychologists, and behavioral specialists who may not find an article about lesson design relevant. Others may struggle with pedagogical language and data discussions in a scholarly journal.

Imagine that, instead, administrators had created a choice board with multiple means of representation. Before the meeting, you receive an email about the purpose of your time together and are given access to a digital choice board, like the one in Table 1. This would replace the need for teachers scrambling for highlighters and reading glasses. Wouldn't it result in a more meaningful meeting?

Lastly, UDL calls for teachers to provide multiple means of action and expression so learners have opportunities to share their progress as they work toward firm goals. Students often have to share their learning in a one-size-fits-all way. Take, for example, the national

1 Anne Meyer, David Gordon, and David H. Rose, *Universal Design for Learning: Theory and Practice* (Wakefield, MA: CAST Professional Publishing, 2015).

Table 1: A Choice Board with Multiple Means of Representation

Read Something	Listen to Something
Choose one or more of the following articles to prepare for the discussion. Read it alone or find some colleagues and read it aloud together.	Choose one of the following podcasts. You can put on your walking shoes and earbuds and listen while doing laps in the hallway!
Watch Something	**Put It in Action**
Pop some popcorn and have a viewing party. These videos will help you learn more to prepare for the discussion.	Choose one of the following ideas and put it into action. You can work alone or find a buddy! You can share your experiences in the discussion.

art standards, which require students to perceive and analyze artistic work. When both of us were in art class, we would examine the same painting and then complete an assessment. Maybe we had to write a five-paragraph essay, make a class presentation, or record a video analyzing the artist's work. It wasn't up to us to decide. The instructor made the decision. That was a lot of work for our teachers to clarify directions, create exemplars, and provide feedback while we sat passively waiting for instructions on what to do. It doesn't have to be this way.

When we unpack our standards, we can determine acceptable evidence and then honor our students and allow them to choose the best way to share their learning as they work together to clarify the purpose of the assignment, discuss their strategies, and share their learning. Imagine how much more engaged students would be if they could choose the artwork and then share their analysis in a written response, a class presentation, or a podcast after working in small groups to decide on the best pathway.

It may seem that some standards do not allow for this level of flexibility, but we are confident there is always a place to shift autonomy and decision-making to the learner. If the firm goal is to write informational text, for example, then all students will, in fact, write. Students can choose to handwrite, type, or use voice-to-text. They may have the option to work with peers or use tools like graphic organizers and sentence stems. The power of UDL is in recognizing variability, articulating firm goals, and shifting decision-making to students to foster expert learning. This release of responsibility is most effective when teachers plan instruction using UDL in a blended learning model.

The power of UDL is in recognizing variability, articulating firm goals, and shifting decision-making to students to foster expert learning. This release of responsibility is most effective when teachers plan instruction using UDL in a blended learning model.

Blended Learning and Complex Coffee Orders

Catlin

As a coffee lover, the explosion of coffee shops, thanks in large part to Starbucks, has made it easy for me to get my daily caffeine fix almost anywhere, anytime. The first Starbucks drive-throughs opened when I was in high school. Now it seems like there is a Starbucks on every other corner. My access to customized caffeinated beverages has increased exponentially in the last twenty years!

Before the Starbucks mobile app changed my coffee ordering habits forever, I would patiently stand in line waiting to place my order. I would listen to people in front of me order. "I'd like a white chocolate mocha with whipped cream." "I'll have a pumpkin spice almond milk latte with caramel drizzle on top." "Can I have a blonde roast with room for cream?" The variety of options and the ability to personalize my coffee order never struck me as unusual. As long as I had been drinking coffee, I had been able to personalize my experience. It wasn't until a trip to Michigan to visit my grandparents that I realized my experience with coffee was wildly different from previous generations'.

One morning during my trip, I took my ninety-one-year-old grandfather to Starbucks for coffee. As we stood in line, I asked him, "What do you want?" He raised an eyebrow, looked confused, and said, "A coffee." It struck me then that when my parents and their parents were growing up, coffee was coffee. Now, ordering a coffee requires a unique vocabulary. We can customize every part of our coffee: the size, type of milk, amount of foam, number of espresso shots, and pumps of syrup. Long gone are the days when ordering a coffee was a simple affair where the only question a customer might get is, "Do you want cream or sugar?"

Thanks to the Starbucks app we can find the closest store, place our unique order, get directions, and an estimated time when our order will be ready. The app has given consumers control over their experience from start to finish, and it saves the employees at Starbucks the time it takes to ring up every order manually. Once I have my coffee, I can choose to hang out in the Starbucks chatting with a friend or working on my computer, or simply take my grande nitro in a Venti cup with a large splash of soy milk to go.

Just as Starbucks has shifted control over my coffee experience to me—by offering a variety of locations, drive-through or comfortable indoor seating, and an easy-to-use app that allows me to place my customized order from anywhere at just about any time—blended learning strives to fundamentally shift control over the students' educational experience from teacher to learner. Blended learning gives students *more* control over the time, place, pace, and path of their learning.

This shift is critical when teaching a generation of students who enjoy so much autonomy and agency beyond school. The students walking through our classroom doors are used to placing their own complicated orders for Strawberry Refreshers and peppermint mocha crème Frappuccinos at Starbucks. So, it's likely jarring for them to enter a classroom where everyone is essentially sipping hot black coffee with no opportunity to personalize their experience, decide whether they'd be more successful working alone or with others, or use technology to minimize the complexity of a task. It should not surprise anyone that students do not enjoy that experience.

Learning, like coffee, is most enjoyable when the consumer (yes, students are the consumers in education!) gets to play an active role in the experience. Learner variability means that different students are going to enjoy learning in different ways, and those preferences are likely to change day to day, just as my coffee order is impacted by my level of exhaustion or the temperature outside. Instead of approaching learning from the perspective that one experience is a good fit for a diverse group of students, blended learning seeks to give students opportunities to control key aspects of their learning.

The Power of Blended Learning

Let's start with a clear definition, since the phrase "blended learning" has been thrown around a lot in the last two years, but it isn't always anchored in a clear definition. Blended learning is the combination of active, engaged learning online with active, engaged learning offline with the goal of giving students more control over the time, place, pace, and path of their learning experience.

We believe the most important part of this definition is "active, engaged learning." Ultimately, the goal of blended learning is to shift students to the center of the learning process. This demands that they play an active role. *They* must be the ones thinking, doing, discussing, collaborating, problem-solving, creating, and reflecting. We recognize that this is a much more cognitively and socially demanding role for students who may be comfortable passively consuming information and observing their teachers doing the work in a lesson. The truth is that it is much easier to be a student in a teacher-centered classroom and much more challenging to be a student in a student-centered classroom. Yet the skills and habits students hone when *they* are doing the work and *they* are driving their learning experiences in directions that are meaningful, interesting, and relevant to them will serve them long after they leave our classrooms.

There are many different ways to combine this active, engaged learning online and offline, which is why there are a variety of blended learning models and strategies, as pictured in Table 2.

The original taxonomy of blended learning models is evolving as educators experiment with different ways of combining online and offline learning. For example, choice boards can be composed of entirely offline activities, which would not fall under the umbrella of blended learning. By contrast, a teacher can create a choice board of online and offline learning activities that position the student as an active agent. That case would absolutely be considered a blended learning strategy. Similarly, the 5Es instructional model—which was initially designed for encouraging student-led inquiry in science classrooms—can also be used to combine active engaged learning online and offline, making it a robust blended learning model.

Not only do these blended learning models work well in a physical classroom, they also work well entirely online, or in a blend of the two. We've long known blended learning could work in classrooms

Table 2: Blended Learning Rotation Models

Blended Learning Models and Strategies

The Whole-Group Rotation Model

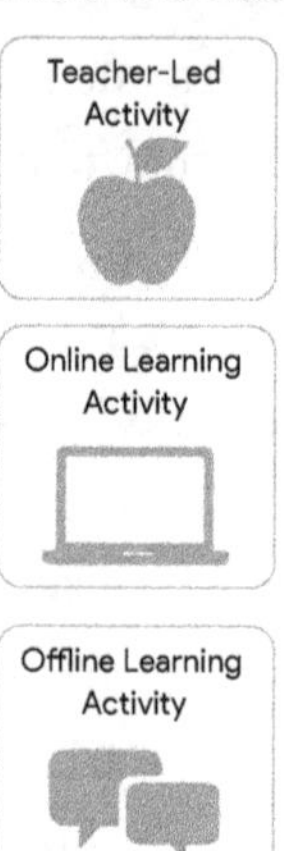

The entire class rotates between online and offline learning activities that attempt to balance the online with the offline and the individual with the collaborative to maximize the power and potential of the learning community while leveraging technology to create personalized pathways. While students are working online, the teacher is free to work with individuals or small groups of learners who need more instruction, modeling, guided practice, feedback, or support.

Example:

- Teachers can begin class with offline retrieval practice to help students revisit previous concepts or skills or anticipate new ones.
- Then they can transition the class online and give students the option to explore information presented in a text or video, depending on their preference.
- Once students have had the opportunity to self-pace through that information, the teacher can provide additional instruction or guide an interactive modeling session.
- After the direct instruction and modeling, the teacher can allow students to decide whether to practice and apply learning online with a computer program or offline with a partner.

The Station Rotation Model

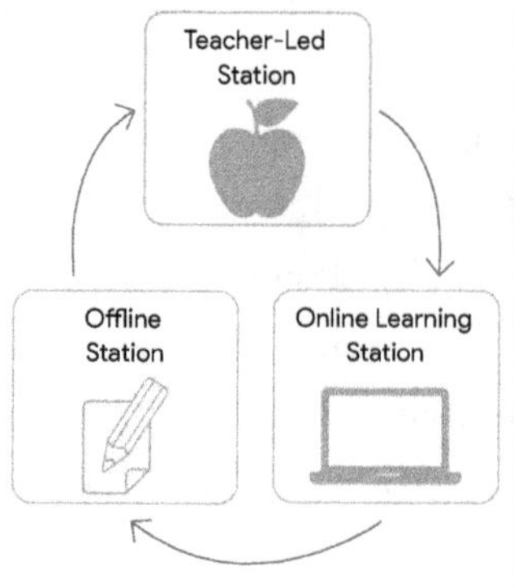

Small groups of students rotate through a series of stations or learning activities that combine offline and online learning. Typically, a station rotation includes a teacher-led station, online stations, and offline stations. This model frees the teacher to work with small groups of learners to more effectively differentiate instruction, models, supports, and scaffolds for learners with different needs, abilities, language proficiencies, learning preferences, and interests.

Example:

- The teacher-led station can be focused on onboarding students to a particular strategy or skill using an "I do–We do–Groups do–You do" progression and differentiating the experience for each group.
- The online station can engage students in an asynchronous discussion designed to get them accessing and sharing their prior knowledge on a topic.
- The offline station can ask students to read a text and work with a partner to create a concept map or sketchnote.

Flipped Classroom

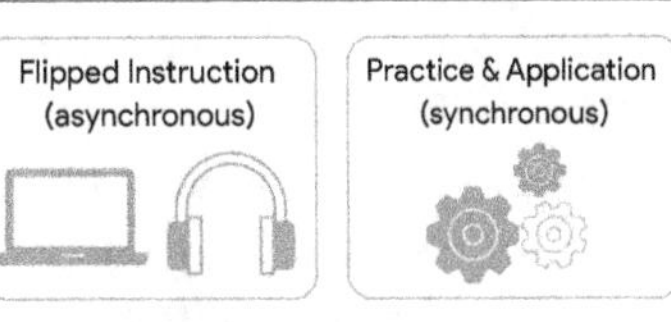

Teachers use video strategically to shift instruction online, where students can self-pace through explanations, pausing, rewinding, and rewatching as needed. Students can manipulate the video instruction by slowing down the video or adding captions to increase accessibility. Teachers can spend more time supporting students as they take what they've learned and attempt to apply it.

Example:

- Prior to the video, teachers may want to pre-teach vocabulary to remove any barriers to accessing the information in the video or present a "hook activity" to pique student interest in the topic.
- Teachers can record a mini-lesson explaining a concept (e.g., kinetic energy) using a mix of text and visuals. They can wrap the video in an Edpuzzle lesson that prompts students to answer specific questions about the content of the video or pair the video with a guided note template.
- After students have seen the video, teachers can strategically pair or group students for a follow-up activity that challenges them to apply what they learned in the video.

Playlist/Individual Rotation

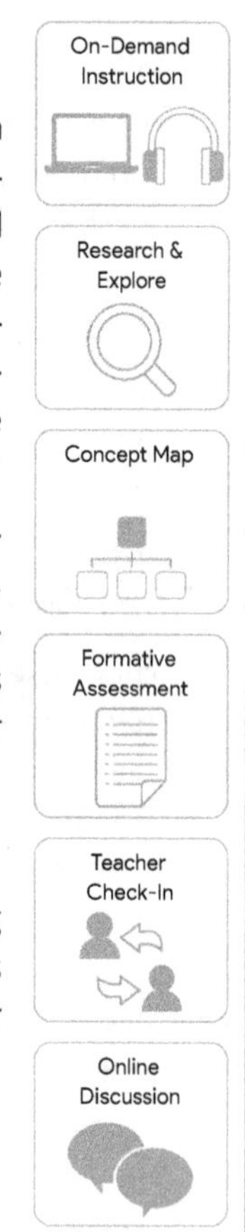

A playlist is a series of learning activities presented in a sequence, moving learners toward a desired outcome or learning objective. Playlists have on-demand instruction and models, combine online and offline learning activities, provide meaningful choices, and—ideally—provide teachers with opportunities to conference with students as they progress through the playlist.

During these conferences, teachers can review formative assessment data, discuss student progress, and modify individual playlists. Playlists can be differentiated for groups of learners at different levels of readiness and can be personalized via teacher check-ins throughout the process.

Example:

- Teachers can create a sequence of learning activities to guide students through the process of learning about fractions, writing an essay, or completing a multi-step performance task.

Choice Boards

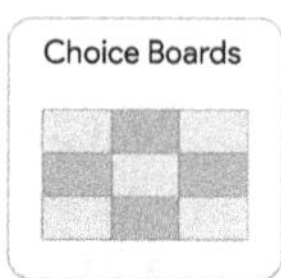

Choice boards can be organized to provide students with a mix of online and offline activities that target specific standards, skills, processes, vocabulary, etc. The goal is to allow students to choose the specific activities they think they will enjoy and benefit from spending time on. As students self-pace through items on a choice board, the teacher is freed to work with individual students or small groups. They can use the time created by a choice board to conference with students or conduct side-by-side assessments of completed work.

Example:

- Teachers may create a choice board designed to support review and practice, targeting specific skills, concepts, and vocabulary. Alternatively, they can create a standards-aligned board to provide students with meaningful choices about how they engage with a particular standard or skill.

using the rotation models highlighted in Table 2. However, we were thrilled by how well these models also worked when students were learning remotely from home.

Even the station rotation model, which many educators assume must take place in a classroom where they can arrange physical stations, worked beautifully online. During the pandemic, educators used the station rotation model to break a class into smaller groups, making time for small-group instruction. Teachers used the main room in video conferencing sessions to work with a small group at their "teacher-led station," differentiating instruction, leading interactive modeling sessions, facilitating small-group discussions, and providing feedback on student work. Depending on the nature of the online station, students worked asynchronously through an activity or joined a collaborative breakout room to work with their peers on a shared task. The offline station allowed students to log off the video call, take a break from the screen, and engage with a tactile or experiential task. For example, students might go outside and make observations, perform fieldwork to gather data, interview a family member, complete pencil-and-paper practice, or create a concept map. The possibilities were limitless!

The flexibility of these blended learning models is exciting, because it means teachers do not need one skill set to design and facilitate learning in a classroom and another skill set to work with students online. Instead, teachers who develop confidence using blended learning models to design accessible, inclusive, and equitable learning experiences can traverse any teaching and learning landscape.

UDL and Blended Learning: The Ultimate Power Couple

Think about the great power couples of our time: Michelle and Barack, Beyoncé and Jay-Z, William and Kate, Neil Patrick Harris and David Burtka. What do all power couples have in common? They complement each other and balance each other out. They have individual strengths and different vulnerabilities. They respect and support one another, making each part stronger. That's what UDL and blended learning do for each other.

UDL makes it crystal clear that learners are wonderfully diverse and that a diversity of experience, skills, interests, and preferences strengthen a learning community, leading to a richer and more dynamic learning experience. That diversity also demands that we—as architects of learning experiences—strive to make learning accessible, inclusive, and equitable by prioritizing flexible pathways and meaningful choices. Teachers fundamentally understand the value of the beliefs at the core of UDL, but they may not be sure how to actualize these beliefs and put them into practice in ways that are sustainable. That is where the other part of this power couple can help! Blended learning provides concrete structures teachers can use to design learning experiences that shift control to learners and create more time for teachers to work directly with individual students or small groups.

The point we want to make in this book is that blended learning is flexible and offers educators several sustainable ways to operationalize the beliefs at the core of UDL. It may feel daunting at first to consider designing and facilitating learning experiences that honor learner variability, provide flexible pathways toward firm goals, and cultivate expert learners. But it's only intimidating if we continue to plan a single experience for the entire class that demands the teacher do the lion's share of the work in the lesson. We encourage teachers to partner with their students and share the responsibility for learning with them.

Blended learning can free the teacher from the role of "expert at the front of the room" and allow them to embrace more sustainable teaching practices so they spend more time in their role as facilitators, working directly with students to support their individual progress toward firm goals. Blended learning without a firm grounding in UDL principles can result in shallow technology use and lackluster learning experiences. UDL without blended learning can make designing flexible pathways feel overwhelming and unsustainable. Together, they pack a powerful punch and like any good power couple function to make each other stronger.

Blended learning without a firm grounding in UDL principles can result in shallow technology use and lackluster learning experiences. UDL without blended learning can make designing flexible pathways feel overwhelming and unsustainable. Together, they pack a powerful punch and like any good power couple function to make each other stronger.

Let's examine some of the synergy between UDL and blended learning.

Learner Variability and Flexible Pathways

We've established that learners are different and will not all travel from point A to point B effectively along the same path. Universally designed blended learning prioritizes student agency as a vehicle to honor this variability and allows students the opportunity to choose the best "path." For example, students will vary in their preferences when it comes to acquiring new information. If the goal is to have students understand the parts of a process, some students will prefer to read, others will enjoy watching a video, and others may enjoy listening to an audio recording or podcast. As they process or make sense of what they've read, watched, or listened to, they might find it helpful to create a concept map, engage in a discussion, or respond to a writing prompt. The more choices a learner has in a given learning experience, the less likely they are to encounter barriers that stall their progress.

But offering these choices may feel overwhelming in the context of a teacher-led whole-group lesson. Instead, using blended learning models, like the playlist model, or strategies, like a choice board, allows for more student control over the time, pace, and path of their experience. This makes offering options more manageable. For example, a teacher can create a math playlist designed to help students construct graphs. The playlist may present information in a variety of formats—text, video, interactive websites—and allow students to select the resource they think they'll have the most success accessing. It can include activities, like analyzing and discussing misleading graphs, and inviting students to decide whether they'd like to participate in a live chat with a partner or post their ideas to an online discussion board. The playlist can also include options for how students practice and apply what they are learning. Some students may prefer to graph online using a platform like Desmos, while others may prefer the tactile experience of graphing on paper. The goal of the playlist is to shift control over the pace of their progress to the learner while providing them with various pathways through the material.

Expert Learners

UDL is grounded in the belief that all students can and should become expert learners. Because blended learning requires that learners take an active role in the learning process, it is important for them to be resourceful, strategic, motivated, and self-aware. Together UDL and blended learning can help students develop the characteristics of an expert learner, because learning is a shared endeavor, or partnership, between the teacher and the learners. The more teachers release responsibility to learners (over time and with lots of scaffolding!), the more opportunities students have to understand themselves as learners and select strategies and pathways that will help them succeed in navigating learning tasks. Through metacognitive skill building, conferencing with teachers, seeking feedback from peers, and engaging in regular reflection, students can develop the skills and attributes needed to be expert learners, which will allow them to thrive in our classrooms and beyond.

Workflows That Actually Work

Ultimately, we believe that the traditional workflows in education don't actually work for anyone. First, they create mountains of paperwork that teachers feel compelled to grade, which robs them of the time and energy they need to design dynamic student-centered learning experiences. Second, these ineffective workflows steal precious time in class when teachers should be working alongside individuals and small groups of learners, supporting their progress toward firm goals. Finally, they cheat students out of the opportunity to take active roles in the learning process, drive their learning in directions that feel interesting and relevant, and become expert learners.

The goal of this book is to reimagine a collection of traditional workflows that are not working. We will weave together the beliefs at the core of UDL and the principles guiding the implementation of

UDL with blended learning models to help teachers shift students to the center of every learning experience. Instead of asking, "How can I?" we want you to ask, "How can *my students*?" This simple shift can help us to establish new workflows that are more sustainable and lighten the teacher's load while actively engaging students in every part of the learning process.

WRAP-UP

UDL and blended learning are indeed the education power couple. Traditional approaches to teaching and learning overburden teachers and prevent students from building autonomy and agency in their learning. What was previously unimaginable becomes possible when we leverage best practices, use innovative technology solutions, and co-create learning experiences with students.

When we transfer the power of design, decision-making, and collaboration to the learners we serve, we create spaces that allow them to build skills necessary for success in any pathway they choose to pursue. Just as important, we create a more balanced workload for ourselves as we aren't doing work for students that they are capable of doing themselves.

REFLECT AND DISCUSS

1. We know classrooms are composed of a wide spectrum of needs, abilities, preferences, identities, and interests. Why do you think so many teachers still design a single whole-group lesson for such a diverse group of learners? What makes it challenging for teachers to honor learner variability in the design of their lessons?
2. If expert learners are motivated, resourceful, strategic, and self-aware, what changes need to happen in classrooms to help students develop these attributes?

3. Which blended learning models have you used with students? How have you prioritized student agency using those models?
4. What synergies do you see between UDL and blended learning? How do you see them working together to create more accessible, inclusive, and equitable learning experiences?

PUTTING IT INTO PRACTICE

As we embark on this journey to explore new, more sustainable workflows, think about your current approach to instruction, feedback, grading, etc. and identify a workflow that isn't working well. Describe that workflow in writing, a video recording, or in a conversation with a colleague.

- What are you currently doing?
- What parts of it are working? Which are not and why aren't they?
- How is this workflow creating imbalance in your teaching life?
- Once you've identified an unsustainable workflow, ask, "How can *my students* ________?" and reimagine this workflow, positioning the student to do the work.
- How might your students take an active and engaged role in this workflow?
- How can you release responsibility for this workflow and help students take the lead?
- What support or scaffolding might they need to successfully lead this revised workflow?
- How might asking your students to actively engage impact their learning or the culture in your classroom? How might this shift help them develop as expert learners?
- Once you have reimagined this workflow, share the idea with your colleagues or personal learning network for feedback.

WORKFLOW SHIFT #1

From Transfer of Information to Student Discovery

Teaching Our Students to Fish

Katie

When I prepared dinner tonight, I was running on fumes. I tried to trick my brain into being awake by sipping on an iced latte and blasting ABBA's "Dancing Queen" throughout the kitchen. "It will be worth it," I told myself. "Family dinner time will make it worth it. And tonight is tacos. Everyone loves tacos, right?"

As you can imagine, this story is already starting out a little like the children's classic *The Little Red Hen*. If you've never read it, here is the gist: A little red hen works her feathers off growing wheat, harvesting the wheat, making flour, and baking bread. And no one wants to help her. Then the ungrateful chicks just expect to roll out and enjoy a nice baguette.

I was sweating in the kitchen like the Little Red Hen trying to do it all when the smell of dinner summoned the kids from their rooms. All at once, the four of them came barreling into the kitchen. Within five seconds, someone announced, "Tacos again? All we evvvvvver eat is tacos."

Suddenly, my kitchen was in a full dress rehearsal of an off-Broadway show titled *Tacos Are Gross and We Never Get to Eat What We Want.* A perfect harmony of complaining and disarray. I had seen this musical before, and I was ready for my part. I aggressively jabbed a tortilla chip into a bowl of queso and used my best—and kindest—teacher voice to explain to my dear children that they normally love tacos. I was wrist deep in queso when my husband launched into "I'm Not Mad. I'm Just Disappointed." End scene.

My dinner scene reminds me of an old adage: "Give someone a fish and they will eat for a day. Teach them to fish and they will eat for a lifetime." It's a lovely sentiment, but I want to revise it. It's time to take out the sewing machine and embroider an apron that says, "Give someone a fish and they will eat it if it meets their dietary needs and they're in the mood for it. Teach them to find food and cook and they can make their own meals."

We are spending too much time preparing lessons and delivering instruction with the intention of "feeding" knowledge to our students. Despite our best efforts and an incredible amount of unsustainable energy, our kids, like my own children, look at what we put on their proverbial plates and decide they're going to skip dinner or—at the very least—complain about the meal.

As teachers and practicing graduate instructors, Catlin and I discuss that we are doing too many things for learners that they are capable of doing themselves. And—more devastating?—our efforts haven't resulted in our desired impact. Student engagement is low, opportunity gaps persist, and teachers are exhausted.

We have to figure out how to make this work more sustainable for educators, and we also have to make it more meaningful for our learners. If we can design instruction so we teach our learners to fish, we can shift control and power to honor them, and we can increase ownership, autonomy, pride, and outcomes.

As I connect with my colleagues, read blogs, and work with thousands of educators around the world, I acknowledge their pain. Educators are overwhelmed, drained, and often feel absolutely left out to sea. The waters are choppy, our nets are heavy, and we can't feed all our learners with a single fishing pole. Instead, we have to design learning experiences that teach *students* how to understand their dietary needs, find ingredients, create recipes, and ultimately, discover how to feed themselves. Then, and only then, can we eat our queso in peace.

The Research and Reality: Galatea versus Golem

A recent research study aptly titled "Learner-Centered Design: Is Sage on the Stage Obsolete?" confirms what we believe to be true about education:

> The instructor's role in a TC [teacher-centered] classroom is to be the expert who disseminates information to students usually using a lecture teaching methodology. Students have had years of experiences with TC learning environments and have come to believe it is the responsibility of the instructor to take control of the teaching. The advantage of teachers maintaining the expert role is the respect given by students for sharing their expertise in class lectures. The disadvantage of teacher as expert is that students rely on the instructor to disseminate information and can be intimidated to take ownership of their own knowledge creation.[1]

1 Sheri Stover, Sharon Heilmann, and Amelia Hubbard, "Learner-Centered Design: Is Sage on the Stage Obsolete?," *Journal of Effective Teaching in Higher Education* 1, no. 1 (November 3, 2018): 3.

There is some serious Psychology 101 going on here, so let's unpack it. If your classroom is teacher-directed, you take the responsibility for the design of instruction and the transfer of information to students. This influences students. They internalize that it is the teacher's job to share information, and it's the students' job to observe their own education. If we are lucky, they will choose to engage or play along and comply, but as is happening more and more often, they retreat or ignore the instruction completely, leaving us to give a performance to an audience of passive observers. Then, when they don't learn, the blame is placed on us. After all, we are the ones sharing the information, right? Not anymore, kiddos.

> *If your classroom is teacher-directed, you take the responsibility for the design of instruction and the transfer of information to students. This influences students. They internalize that it is the teacher's job to share information, and it's the students' job to observe their own education.*

When we rely solely on teacher-centered instruction, we create a self-fulfilling prophecy. To continue our psych lesson, we'll say that self-fulfilling prophecies can have positive or negative outcomes. The positive effects are called *Galatea effects.* In the Greek myth that the Galatea effect gets its name from, the sculptor Pygmalion creates a statue of a woman. He names her Galatea and falls in love with her. His desire for Galatea is so strong that he infuses her with life, and all ends happily. Negative expectancy effects are called *Golem effects.* In Jewish folklore, the Golem was an inanimate creature given life to serve its creator. But the monster became dangerous and had to be destroyed.[2]

2 Elisha Y. Babad, Jacinto Inbar, and Robert Rosenthal, "Pygmalion, Galatea, and the Golem: Investigations of Biased and Unbiased Teachers," *Journal of Educational Psychology* 74, no. 4 (August 1982): 459–74.

Overreliance on teachers must be destroyed! (Too dramatic?) It is frustrating that students don't take more initiative for their own learning, but the models we use actually prevent students from taking ownership. And that is Golem-y. From a practical perspective, you are doing all the work, delivering whole-class instruction to learners—instruction that you are staying up until 2:00 a.m. to design. As a result, students come to believe it is your job to do all of the work. You are exhausted, and students are disengaged or excluded. That is a bad deal all around.

If you're doing all the work to identify problems and design lessons while students don't have the opportunity to personalize their learning journeys, you're not leveraging UDL and blended learning yet. If all students are different and need different levels of challenge, how can one learn to identify challenging goals in a class where everyone has the same goal? How can they learn from mistakes when we design lessons that end once mistakes are made? How can we expect students to fight and persevere to understand when the work is one-size-fits-all? How can we expect students to solve problems if we don't let them choose which problems to tackle?

If we want to meet the needs of all learners, especially those from historically marginalized groups, it is critical that we commit to "firm goals, flexible means" and design student-centered instruction to change expectations within the classroom and around learning in general. UDL is a framework that recognizes that there are many ways to reach the same goal, and blended learning models provide teachers with multiple paths to provide that flexibility for learners. When educators allow students to take ownership of and self-differentiate their learning, every student sees a personalized pathway where they can be successful. Bring on the Galatea effects!

The four core curriculum components of UDL include firm goals and flexible methods, materials, and assessments. There are many ways for students to learn content under study, many materials that can support students in their zone of proximal development, and numerous pathways for students to express what they have learned when we shift our workflow from the good ole sage on the stage (instructor) to the guide on the side (facilitator). Granted, this requires a significant shift in the way that curriculum is designed and delivered, but UDL and blended learning provide us with evidence-based frameworks to do this work.

When educators allow students to take ownership of and self-differentiate their learning, every student sees a personalized pathway where they can be successful.

Obviously, there is a huge win for teachers when they aren't the only ones carrying the cognitive load of instruction, but there are significant positive outcomes for learners as well. Research shows that there are significant academic, behavioral, and social-emotional benefits to students when we shift to a model of discovery. In student-centered classrooms, learners experience increased academic outcomes, higher levels of inclusiveness, increased self-esteem, reduced anxiety, a more positive attitude toward instructors, deeper relationships with peers, and feelings of social solidarity.[3] We can't imagine a single teacher reading that who doesn't say, "Yes, please! I want those outcomes!"

In this chapter, we offer three ways to shift the workflow from the model that is predominantly teacher-directed to one where students take charge of their own learning.

3 Sheri Stover, Sharon Heilmann, and Amelia Hubbard, "Learner-Centered Design," 1–19.

Strategy #1: Embrace the Choice Board

Student agency is an essential aspect of blended learning. It requires that we design our lessons to offer students meaningful choices. These choices can help us universally design learning experiences that strive to remove barriers and invite students to decide how to engage with information, make meaning, and share their learning.

You can design choice boards for a variety of purposes or learning objectives, but teachers looking to shift students into the driver's seat when it comes to discovery can create a choose-your-learning-path choice board, like the one pictured in Figure 1, to allow students to acquire information, make meaning, and share their learning in ways that feel accessible.

Figure 1: Choose-Your-Learning-Path Choice Board

Choose Your Learning Path Adventure Choice Board		
Acquire Information	Make Meaning	Share Your Learning

A choose-your-learning-path adventure is ideal for introducing a new topic, concept, process, or issue. Elementary teachers can introduce topics like animal habitats, weather patterns, or famous people from history using this strategy. Secondary teachers may want to introduce a genre of writing or an art movement, a process like cell division, or issues like censorship or voting laws. However, instead of the teacher frontloading the learning with a presentation, lecture, mini-lesson, or demonstration, the goal is to allow students to explore resources and select strategies *they* think will help them to learn about the subject of the choice board.

To prepare a choose-your-learning-path adventure with a choice board, teachers will want to decide on the path they want to use. You may want to begin with one of the following:

- Acquire information–Make meaning–Share your learning
- Engage–Explore–Explain
- Activate prior knowledge–Acquire new information–Apply your learning

Once you select a clear path, each column in your choice board will correspond to a step in that path. It's important to remember that blended learning models and strategies are flexible! So, you can create as many columns in your choice board as you want. You are not limited to three, so feel free to modify and adjust these paths to work for you and your students! If you are an elementary science teacher who loves the 5Es instructional model, you can create a choice board using the 5Es (engage, explore, explain, elaborate, evaluate) to have students engage with a question like "Why do objects move?" or to learn about a topic like photosynthesis.

As you design your choice board, regardless of the path you use to structure it, you will want to focus on keeping the choices varied so they appeal to students with different learning preferences. If you are asking them to acquire new information, you may want to curate a collection of physical or digital texts, videos, podcasts, or interactive websites. As students shift to making meaning, some may prefer more tactile experiences like practicing offline, completing a graphic organizer, or creating a flowchart or concept map; others may prefer a writing or reflection prompt to consider and respond to; and others will enjoy engaging in conversation with a classmate or group of peers to make sense of the information they read, watched, or listened to in the "acquire information" stage of the choice board. Finally, you can ask students to select a strategy for sharing their learning that feels most comfortable to them. Perhaps you invite them to record a short video or audio explanation, draw sketchnotes, perform a skit, or construct a model to share their learning. The possibilities are endless! In fact, you can even have a "your choice" square in the final column to allow students to decide on a strategy they want to use to communicate what they learned.

The goal at each stage of a choose-your-learning-path adventure is to give students meaningful choices to remove barriers and help them tackle tasks with a higher level of confidence in their ability to be successful. They can complete the items on a choice board individually, with a partner, or as part of a group, depending on their preference.

We love the versatility of choice boards, which will be evident from the number of choice boards we have featured throughout this book! They effectively shift students to the center of the learning experience by inviting them to decide how to spend their time and energy. This increased student autonomy and agency also frees you to invest your time and energy working alongside students.

Strategy #2: Leverage Reciprocal Teaching and Jigsaw Activities

There are numerous strategies teachers can leverage to put students in charge of learning and teaching each other. Two of these models are reciprocal teaching and the jigsaw method. Both can be universally designed to ensure all learners have opportunities to become experts in collaborative learning. Both models begin with a collaborative group, ideally of four students, which makes this model perfect for a station rotation model. But the groups can also work through a playlist collaboratively, checking in with the teacher at predetermined checkpoints.

Reciprocal Teaching

Reciprocal teaching is an inclusive practice where students work collaboratively to make sense of a shared text. A highly adaptable strategy, it can be used with a range of students and content at all levels of development—elementary to secondary to adults.[4] For example, students may be assigned a short profound text in English language arts or world language, a primary source document in social studies, a piece of music in chorus, or a peer-reviewed scientific journal in physics. Using the principles of UDL, teachers ensure the text is accessible by providing printed copies, digital text, and access to audio versions and translations of the text.

The first time you use reciprocal teaching, model the four comprehension strategies: a) summarizing, b) asking questions, c) clarifying or looking up vocabulary, and d) predicting what will happen next. This explicit instruction can be done through a prerecorded video, or you can model the roles in small-group instruction in a station rotation lesson. Read a section of the text and model the four strategies. Once students are familiar with the four strategies, each student in the group is assigned a different comprehension strategy so they are reading with purpose. The four roles are summarizer, questioner, clarifier of vocabulary, and predictor, as shown in Figure 2. Students can switch roles as they work through the text so they have practice with each of the strategies. The strategy can be adapted when there are eight members in each group. In that case, two members are assigned to each comprehension strategy so they can collaborate and share ideas before sharing with the larger group. If there is

4 Ruth McAllum, "Reciprocal Teaching: Critical Reflection on Practice," *Kairaranga* 15, no. 1 (2014): 26–35.

an uneven number of students in a group, pair up two students who would benefit from additional peer support and ask them to work together using the same comprehension strategy.

Figure 2: Reciprocal-Teaching Comprehension Strategies

Reciprocal Teaching		
Predictor	Make three predictions as you read and support each one with a detail from the text.	
Summarizer	Identify the most important points made in the reading. Then summarize what you learned, making connections between the important points.	
Questioner	Be aware of what you wonder as you read this text and capture those wonderings in 3–5 thought-provoking questions.	
Clarifier	Identify three vocabulary words, concepts, or statements in the text that were unclear and ask questions about them.	

Research argues that all students are able to participate more fully and independently in learning activities when reciprocal teaching is used with flexible and diverse groups of students.[5]

Jigsaw Activities

Reciprocal teaching is sometimes used interchangeably with the jigsaw method, but they are not the same. Jigsawing is when a student or group of students specialize in a topic, and they then teach others. In a jigsaw, a teacher can chunk instruction into four parts. There may be four sections in a chapter, four chapters in a text, four math problems, four vocabulary words, four steps in a process, or four stretches to learn in a physical education class.

Figure 3: Jigsaw of the Four Parts of the Scientific Method

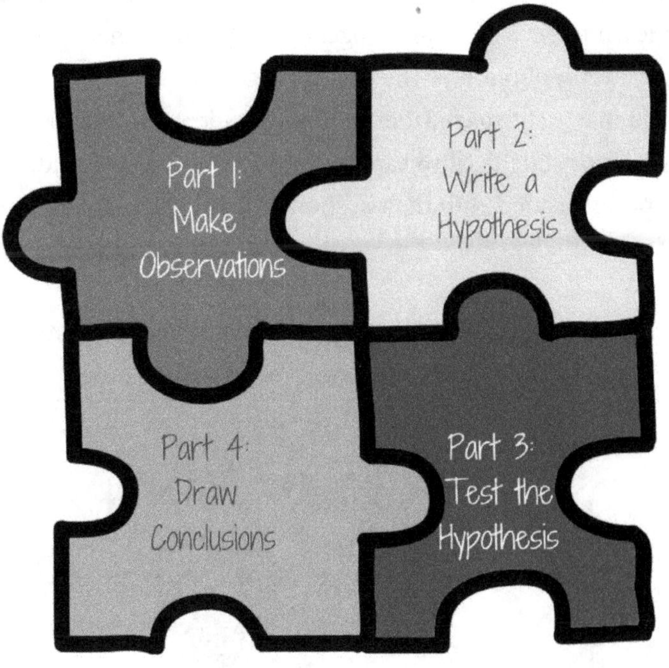

5 Ibid.

Four groups become experts in their specific part, as shown in Figure 3, which focuses on the four steps of the scientific method. Students can build their expertise through reading, watching, observing, conducting research, and engaging in exploration. Students in each group should focus on identifying, defining, and understanding key vocabulary and concepts related to their topic so they can effectively communicate what they've learned to their classmates.

After each group has had time to develop their expertise on their topic—which can happen as part of a station rotation or whole-group rotation lesson—new groups are formed with a mix of students from each group. Just like the pieces of an actual puzzle fit together, students in each of the four subcategories come together to combine what they've learned into a cohesive whole, taking turns teaching each other. This allows all students to step into the role of the teacher to share their knowledge. It challenges them to articulate their learning in a clear and cogent way, listen to their peers, and think critically about how the parts fit together.

You may want to consider grouping students in a shared digital document or slide deck to capture the key vocabulary or ideas and concepts associated with their section of the reading or larger topic, as pictured in Figure 4.

Figure 4: Collaborative Jigsaw Slide Deck Template

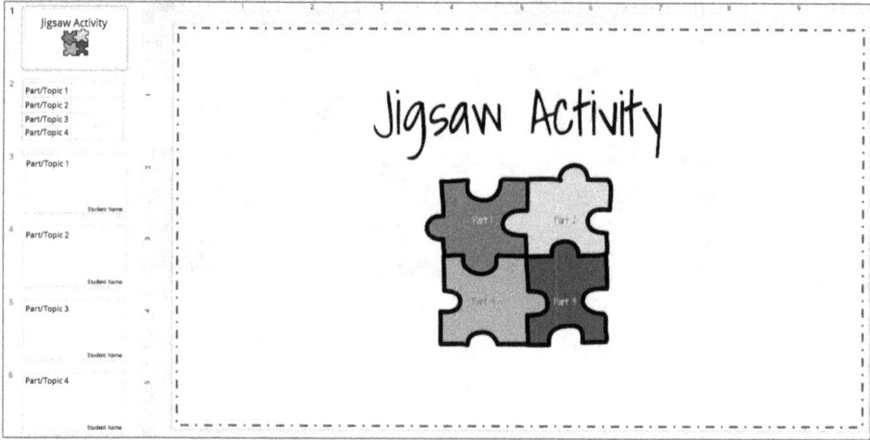

A jigsaw activity relieves pressure from the teacher to cover content via lecture or direct instruction. It also makes it possible to cover more ground in a shorter period of time. We frequently use jigsaw activities with our graduate students to break up dense or lengthy texts and allow them to focus on one section of reading to become the "experts." Then they teach a group of peers and engage in lively discussions about the reading. The feedback from our graduate students has been overwhelmingly positive, since this method lessens their reading load while also providing opportunities for social learning. While groups are sharing their learning, you can observe and listen to identify areas of the topic you may want to spend more time explaining, discussing, or reviewing with students.

Strategy #3: Make Direct Instruction Differentiated and Bite-Sized

We have discussed the importance of moving away from the teacher as the only source of knowledge in the classroom, but this is not to say that teachers cannot provide targeted instruction to learners. Given the significant variability of learners, it is clear that a whole-class lecture will not meet the needs of all learners. Even though the concept of teacher-led instruction may seem counterintuitive to UDL, it does not have to be. One of the UDL guidelines reminds instructors to build fluencies with graduated levels of support for practice and performance.

If we think of learning as a continuum, much like Vygotsky's zone of proximal development,[6] direct instruction is when the level of support is highest. Scaffolding, as a component of direct instruction, is an effective teaching method to increase student comprehension. Vygotsky defined the zone of proximal development as the

6 L. S. Vygotsky, *Mind in Society: The Development of Higher Psychological Processes* (Cambridge, MA: Harvard University Press, 1980).

distance between a learner's actual developmental level and their potential developmental level as determined by the guidance of a more knowledgeable individual. Teachers can provide this guidance and support by scaffolding instruction to small groups of students to supplement student discovery. We recommend providing direct instruction to small groups of students in a station rotation model using a mini-lesson. Although the specifics of a mini-lesson vary, many education experts agree that it should last no more than ten to fifteen minutes and contain four basic components: connection, teaching, active engagement, and link, as in Figure 5.

Connection: Make a connection to the goal of the instruction and the evidence you used to create the group so all learners understand the purpose of the lesson. For example, you might begin with "I reviewed the drafts of your essays, and although you alluded to some of the primary sources, none of you cited any evidence. I created a scaffold and want to share it with you so you can revise your work to align with the rubric."

Teaching: This is a period of direct instruction. Use it as a foundation before encouraging students to personalize the next steps to challenge and support themselves. We don't want students to rely on direct instruction; rather, they should think of small-group instruction as a targeted coaching session. Also, when you are working with a small group, try not to rely on a single representation. For example, if you're providing instruction verbally, use visuals or a multimedia presentation to support it.

Active Engagement: Provide a short period of time for students to do something that will provide informal formative assessment. For example, you could provide an example of a response that cites textual evidence, model how you could revise one section of a response using textual evidence, and then provide an option for students to explain the process to a partner or summarize the process

Figure 5: Small-Group Instruction Mini-lesson Planning Template

Small-Group Instruction: Mini-lesson Planning Template	
Focus standard/skill:	
Learning objective/goal:	
Grouping strategy:	
Connection: • Clearly state the goal of instruction • Explain how you grouped students for this lesson	

Teaching:
• Provide direct instruction and modeling (e.g., I do...)
  ○ Outline steps
  ○ Select problems/prompts at different levels of rigor
  ○ Create necessary scaffolds	

Active engagement: • Guide the group through an example (e.g., We do...) • Strategically pair students for peer practice (e.g., Groups do...) ○ Collect informal data as pairs work	
Link: • Clearly connect back to the goal of the lesson • Assign independent practice (e.g., You do...)	

in writing. You may also prompt each student to revise a section in their own response and give each other feedback. Just ensure that the mini-lesson doesn't have students passively watching without the accountability of a response.

Link: Before the next station rotation, be clear about linking back to the goal and then directing students to applied practice or more independent work. For example, you might say, "Now that you understand how to cite evidence, you are going to review the primary source documents and revise your work. You can choose to work alone or together. Be sure to review the rubric to ensure your work is aligned before you resubmit." Consider taking time for students to create their own goals or summarize what they need so they can work successfully to complete their revisions.

In this small-group mini-lesson, you are transferring the responsibility of learning to the learner, providing them with not just information but a personalized strategy with just-in-time scaffolds. Clearly, the instruction described would not be necessary for students who are effectively citing textual evidence. Focusing on a specific concept, strategy, or skill with students who need it ensures that students are getting what they need while also taking responsibility for their own learning process.

WRAP-UP

As educators, we are experts in our subject areas, but more than that, we are experts in learning. As much as it may seem rewarding to share knowledge and transfer information to students, it simply is not providing us with the outcomes necessary for our learners to be successful in whatever path they choose to pursue. In universally designed blended learning classrooms, we embrace the value of students learning how to be learners as they construct their own knowledge, learn critical collaboration skills, and transfer this self-awareness and self-direction to other aspects of their lives.

As we shared in strategy #3, you can still target instruction in bite-sized amounts for students while your classroom makes it clear that learning is a shared responsibility. You are not solely responsible for transferring knowledge, and the reality is that trying to plan instruction that way leads to too many sleepless nights and heartbreaking outcomes. Embrace your inner Galatea and know that if you design a classroom that expects students to take ownership of their learning, it will become a self-fulfilling prophecy. And then you can take a seat, observe the collaboration, and maybe drink a cup of hot coffee, for once.

REFLECT AND DISCUSS

1. Think about a real-life example of when you've done all the planning and the outcomes were disappointing (like Katie's taco night). Why is it critical to provide options and choices when we design a shared experience?
2. How can you use the choice board structure to encourage student autonomy and agency? How would you format your choice board to encourage student discovery?
3. How can you transition an upcoming lecture or teacher-directed lesson into a student-led experience with the reciprocal teaching strategy or jigsaw model?
4. When you do provide instruction, it is critical that it is targeted and evidence based. How can the station rotation model support student-directed instruction and bite-sized teacher-directed differentiated instruction?

PUTTING IT INTO PRACTICE

Teaching means much more than standing in front of a classroom and lecturing. We can allow students to build background knowledge, explore resources, and learn using a variety of approaches. Often, these approaches are teacher-directed, but when we shift from a lecturer to a designer, we can help students build ownership and autonomy. Choose one of the strategies outlined in this chapter to move toward more student-led learning in your classroom.

- Strategy #1: Embrace the choice board
- Strategy #2: Leverage reciprocal teaching and jigsaw
- Strategy #3: Make direct instruction bite-sized

First, identify a learning objective or desired result to guide your design work.

Next, select the strategy you want to use to shift responsibility for discovering information over to your students.

Take time to consider the following questions:

- What blended learning model will you use to give students more control over the time, place, pace, or path of their learning?
- How will you use your time during the lesson to maximize your impact?
- What formative assessment data will you collect to measure student understanding and comprehension?
- How will you ensure students have flexible pathways? Where can you provide meaningful choices to remove barriers?

Once you've had time to think about those questions, draft a lesson that positions the students to take the lead in discovering information. Create any supports and scaffolds students might need to be successful.

Planning Template 1: Student Discovery Lesson

Learning objective or desired result: • What would you like students to know, understand, or be able to do at the end of this lesson? • What skills would you like them to develop as a result of working through this learning activity?	
Select the strategy you want to use to shift responsibility for discovering information over to your students. • Choose-your-learning-path choice board • Reciprocal teaching strategy • Jigsaw model • Bite-sized, differentiated small-group instruction	
Take time to consider the following questions: • What blended learning model will you use to give students more control over the time, place, pace, or path of their learning? • How will you use your time during the lesson to maximize your impact? • What formative assessment data will you collect to measure student understanding and comprehension? • How will you ensure students have flexible pathways? Where can you provide meaningful choices to remove barriers?	
Outline your lesson overview. Include information on the following: • How will you group students? • What steps will students move through? • What supports and scaffolds will they need? • What mechanisms are embedded in the lesson to collect formative assessment data?	

WORKFLOW SHIFT #2

From Whole-Group Teacher-Led to Small-Group Student-Led Discussion

No More Swimming in Chocolate

Katie

In the book *Unlearning: Changing Your Beliefs and Your Classroom with UDL*, Allison Posey and I discuss the unlearning cycle, a journey we all consistently take that moves us in a pattern of learn, unlearn, and relearn.[1] One of the best sentence frames to capture an unlearning cycle is "I used to think ________________, then I thought ____________________, but now I think ____________________." I'll show you how it works.

I used to think that *Willy Wonka & the Chocolate Factory* painted a colorful picture of a candy utopia. When I was a kid, I dreamed of swimming in the chocolate fountain, shrinking along with Mike Teavee, and getting a taste of the everlasting gobstopper. Willy Wonka's chocolate factory was a fantasy world. As I got a little older, I thought it was weird that he invited six random kids to his home with the intention of "gifting" one of them his whole factory. I mean, that seems like a lot of responsibility for a nine-year-old.

1 Allison Posey and Katie Novak, *Unlearning: Changing Your Beliefs and Your Classroom with UDL* (Wakefield, MA: CAST Professional Publishing, 2020).

Now that I'm an adult, I think the idea of swimming through warm chocolate fudge is a thing of nightmares. Alas, unlearning.

I feel the same way about classroom discussions. I used to think that, as a teacher, it was my job to conduct a classroom discussion, posing deep questions on Bloom's taxonomy and calling on students who were leaning at the edge of their seats, arms waving in the air like sails coming to shore. After teaching for a couple of years, I recognized that calling on the same two students all the time was neither a great way to build community nor a particularly effective way to formatively assess student knowledge.

I unlearned the ole "I'll call on you with your hand up" and went for the Popsicle sticks. I can still see myself sitting on a stool in front of the classroom, still asking all the questions, and then gracefully whipping out Popsicle sticks as I called on random students who inevitably gave me one of three answers:

1. The right answer
2. The wrong answer
3. No answer or "Huh?"

Now, if I kept my energy high enough, I could recover from wrong and no answers by giving creative options like "phone a friend" or "I'll come back to you," but I was exhausted. In my memory, I look a little like one of the bingo callers from my memere's church basement bingo games. I pulled out a stick and then yelled out names as if there was a prize: "B-8. B-8. Does anyone have Bingo? Oh, B-8 is absent. Crap. Okay, let's try again. O-75. Does O-75 know the answer?" Legit painful. At the same time I was calling out the ole bingo balls in the classroom, I was also teaching college courses online. When I first started to teach online in 2004, my online discussion followed a pattern like this:

1. I posed a discussion question.
2. Learners would write a response to the discussion question.

3. Learners would need to respond to two other classmates' discussion questions. These responses ranged from multiparagraph narratives to takeaways as profound as "I agree!" or "I like your post."

No better than Bingo calling.

Many, if not all of you, have experienced online education. If you have taken an online course, you are likely familiar with the "discussion board," a place where classmates post original reflections or thoughts and other classmates pain themselves to respond in two hundred characters. I sometimes refer to the discussion board as a place where brilliant ideas go to die. A little dark, I know.

I have been teaching for twenty years, and goodness gracious, I continue to unlearn. When it all started, I used to think that it was my job to ask questions and call on students who knew the answers. Then, I thought it was a better idea to ask the questions and call on random students, keeping them on their sweet little toes. Then, I moved to virtual and thought I could birth a meaningful discussion with an open-ended question and a minimum character limit. Now I think that we need to put students in charge of their own discussions regardless of the learning landscape and take a break from asking all the questions.

The Research and the Reality: From Consumer to Producer

Most research on classroom dialogue is focused on a process often referred to as teacher-student initiation, response, and feedback (IRF), a structure that consists of teacher *initiation* of a posed question, student *response,* and teacher *feedback* on the response.[2] This

2 Christine Howe and Manzoorul Abedin, "Classroom Dialogue: A Systematic Review across Four Decades of Research," *Cambridge Journal of Education* 43, no. 3 (September 2013): 325–56.

workflow puts tremendous pressure on the teacher to formulate questions, facilitate the discussion, and be the sole source of feedback about the quality of responses. Certainly, we are not advocating that we completely eliminate teacher-directed discussions using the IRF model, but an overreliance on them is overburdening teachers and allowing many students to breeze through discussion without having to think critically. In short, we are wallowing in Willy Wonka's chocolate river, and students aren't throwing us any peppermint life preservers.

When we shift toward student-led discussions, we are supporting the development of expert learning as well as critical social-emotional learning skills, including self-awareness, empathy, perspective-taking, and responsible decision-making. The Collaborative for Academic, Social, and Emotional Learning (CASEL) is the mothership for all things social-emotional learning in the United States. The CASEL 5 identifies five areas of competence in social-emotional learning: a) self-awareness, b) self-management, c) social awareness, d) relationship skills, and e) responsible decision-making.

In the "CASEL Guide to Schoolwide Social and Emotional Learning," a section on interactive pedagogy discusses the importance of student-led discussions as a mechanism to build social-emotional competency. The guide notes that although the teacher initially plays a key role in these discussions, acting as guide and facilitator, "The goal is for students to ultimately take ownership of the process by asking one another questions, building on the ideas of their peers, and disagreeing thoughtfully." When students have opportunities to facilitate their own discussions and work in small groups, they have opportunities "to support and challenge one another, developing their relationship and responsible decision-making competencies. They also learn to articulate their ideas, explain material to their peers, and use metacognition for a more active approach to learning. This requires a great deal of social and self-awareness as students work to explain their thinking while remaining open to their peers' perspectives."[3]

In addition to encouraging students to develop their in-person and online communication skills, stretch their metacognitive muscles, and develop both their social and self-awareness, discussions are a vehicle for a community of learners to make meaning and construct knowledge together.[4] Discussions shift students from consumers of other people's ideas to producers of their own, positioning them in the role of active agent in the learning environment. As groups of learners wrestle with new ideas, discussion—in person or online—gives them a space to share their thinking, consider different points of view, make connections, and, ultimately, understand and retain what they are learning.

Discussions are a vehicle for a community of learners to make meaning and construct knowledge together. Discussions shift students from consumers of other people's ideas to producers of their own, positioning them in the role of active agent in the learning environment.

Additionally, research is clear that when students take ownership of small-group discussions, they create an interactive community where the passiveness of whole-class instruction is turned to activeness, as student-led discussions generate greater verbal interaction among students and increased self-efficacy in working with peers.[5]

3 CASEL, "The CASEL Guide to Schoolwide Social and Emotional Learning," accessed March 3, 2022, schoolguide.casel.org/.

4 Karen Swan, "Social Construction of Knowledge and the Community of Inquiry Framework" in *Open and Distance Education Theory Revisited: Implications for the Digital Era*, ed. Insung Jung, 57–65 (Singapore: Springer, 2019).

5 Richard Tan, Ronald Polong, Leila Collates, and Joel Torres, "Influence of Small Group Discussion on the English Oral Communication Self-Efficacy of Filipino ESL Learners in Central Luzon," *TESOL International Journal* 15, no . 1 (2020): 100–106.

Clearly, the benefits of student-led discussions are not spontaneous. As you transition from whole-class models of discussion to student-led discussions, it will be important to scaffold the process and offer feedback to small groups on their interactions by leveraging best practices in UDL and blended learning.

As students assume ownership of their discussions and reflective practices, you can use your teacher-led station in a station rotation to run a small fishbowl discussion, guiding early discussions and offering feedback as students practice their skills. Alternatively, teachers using the whole-group rotation can use offline time to run four-corner conversations with a small group of six to eight students in each corner of the room engaging in a small-group discussion. You can circulate around the room, observing their conversations, capturing formative assessment data using a simple discussion rubric, or simply recording one positive thing you noticed about each group and one thing that would benefit from additional practice. You can share this data with them at the end of the discussion to drive a short reflective practice and goal-setting activity. As students develop their proficiency and confidence engaging in discussion, you can sit back and sip a hot coffee or a Diet Coke and watch the magic unfold, changing the model from IRF to a simple F—feedback. The following strategies can support you in this transition.

Strategy #1: Co-create Norms

If discussions are going to be effective, we need to co-create norms in partnership with our learners. One of our favorite activities to brainstorm norms is from *The Big Book of Tools for Collaborative Teams in a PLC at Work* by Bill Ferriter.[6] The guidance is written for adults, but it can be adapted for younger learners. Before creating participation and discussion norms, encourage learners to complete an activity

6 William M. Ferriter, *The Big Book of Tools for Collaborative Teams in a PLC at Work* (Bloomington, IN: Solution Tree Press, 2020).

called "Sharing Our Pet Peeves and Essential Traits." The directions are simple. Each member should share one pet peeve that they have while working in groups with others and one essential trait that others will notice while working in a group with them. You could ask, for example, what patterns in your own behavior are likely to bother other members of your learning team? Why? What patterns in the behavior of other team members are likely to bother you? Why?

We share our own answers here, but you may decide to make this step anonymous, with students writing answers on an index card, completing a survey, or posting on a virtual Post-it note wall or learning management system (LMS) without including their names.

Catlin

When I am engaged in an in-person discussion, my pet peeve is people who don't make eye contact or respond nonverbally to the speaker. I worry that it comes across as disrespectful and sends the message that they don't care about the person's ideas. This can make people feel unsafe sharing or taking risks in the conversation.

I'm type A and a bit of a Hermione Granger in a discussion—okay, in all things academic! I am extroverted, outspoken, and love to exchange ideas with people! Sometimes I'll jump into the conversation to build on another person's idea, make a connection, or share a different perspective. I have to be careful not to be a "discussion dominator" because I always have so much I want to say. I need to remember the old adage "We have two ears and one mouth so that we can listen twice as much as we speak." I'm still working on that!

Katie

If I am in an in-person discussion, my pet peeve is side conversations. It's not that I mind that people are talking, but I am super distractible (think attention span like a squirrel) and also curious. So, as soon as I see a part of the group start talking, I want in! At this point, I generally become useless to the actual conversation.

One thing you need to know about me is that I love a good tangent. In my head, there is often a connection, but on the surface, you may not see it. In the middle of discussing the importance of inclusive practice in a middle school classroom, I may suddenly remember an amazing story from middle school that I. Have. To. Share. I absolutely see how this can be annoying. But I know this about myself so I encourage anyone on my team to reel me in. My own sister, who I work with, will pantomime pulling in a fish when I get off track so I know immediately that I need to focus!

Once you have peeves and traits out in the open, you can begin to create guidance by answering this question: What are some common actions we will need to take if we are going to make sure that our discussions feel positive and productive to all of our individual members? What actions and behaviors might make people feel unwilling to share their ideas or take risks in a discussion?

Put students in small groups and allow them to draft potential norms or guidance on a document (like the one in Figure 6) so they have shared ownership of the discussion expectations. This can be done in person or as an initial discussion post in an online classroom. It's a great activity to get to know everyone, embrace variability, and build empathy.

Figure 6: Class Agreements for Discussion

Class Agreements for Discussion	
✓ Will do	⊘ Will Avoid
What are some common actions we will need to take if we are going to make sure that our discussions feel positive and productive to all of our individual members?	What actions and behaviors will we avoid because they might make people feel unwilling to share their ideas or take risks in a discussion?

Strategy #2: Scaffolds for the Win

There are numerous barriers to student-led discussions that can be minimized through universally designed scaffolds.

There are numerous barriers to successful student-led discussions that can be minimized through universally designed scaffolds. These scaffolds include giving students options to prepare for discussions ahead of time to ensure more equitable participation, using linguistic supports like sentence stems and sentence frames, and providing discussion techniques or protocols students can use or adapt.

Provide Time to Prep

Many educators are familiar with the peer-to-peer discussion technique called "Think, Pair, Share." This technique is used so often because it acknowledges the importance of time, or preparation, before participating in a discussion. Using a blended learning model, you can provide options and choices for students to prepare for a discussion with the following considerations:

- Provide an overview of the topic of discussion and offer the lesson or unit's essential standards and essential questions. You don't want to craft all discussion questions ahead of time, but students should know the purpose of the discussion and the topics that will be addressed.
- Allow students to meet with their discussion group before the discussion to co-create and review norms and review which protocol they will use for a discussion so they can factor these in when preparing.
- Provide multiple means of representation for students to review the content that will be discussed. You can create a choice board that leverages multimedia resources like podcasts and videos while linking to more traditional texts. Ensuring students have access to the resources necessary to build background knowledge is critical. The choice board can be used to link resources so learners can build background knowledge in preparation for a discussion.
- Provide students with an option to take notes, complete a graphic organizer, or create note cards to organize their ideas as they prepare for the discussion.
- Let the discussion begin! As students participate in discussion, monitor their progress, check in with groups who need more support, and use the outcomes of the discussion as a formative assessment to create groups for an upcoming station rotation.

It may be helpful to provide students with a discussion planning document, as in Figure 7, to guide them through these prediscussion steps.

Figure 7: Discussion-Preparation Document

Discussion-Preparation Document	
Discussion Topic:	
Unit Standards and/or Essential Questions:	
Review our class agreements for discussion. • Identify one thing you want to improve on in this discussion. What goal do you have for yourself in this discussion?	
Select a discussion protocol. • What strategy does your group want to use? • Why did you select this protocol?	
Review the content. • Select a strategy for taking notes about the important information (e.g., traditional notes, concept map, graphic organizer, sketchnotes). • Prepare a list of questions you would like to discuss with your group.	Read | Watch | Listen Discussion questions: 1. 2. 3. 4. 5.

Sentence Frames

When students first begin to collaborate, they may struggle to clearly articulate their ideas and opinions. Providing sentence stems or sentence frames can provide support for students who need it. Over time, students will likely become less reliant on these tools, but having them available may help to make discussions more accessible, especially for students who are English language learners. Table 3 provides examples of sentence frames that can be used to guide discussion. You may want to share these with your students and ask them to offer additional stems.

Table 3: Sentence Stems and Frames to Scaffold Classroom Discussion

Sentence Frames for Discussion	
Check Understanding	_______, could you please rephrase that? I did not understand _______, could you repeat that, please? Can you say more about that? I have a question about _______. [State your question.] I'm not sure I _______. Do you mean _______?
Link Your Comments to the Remarks of Others	My idea is related to _______ idea _______. I really liked _______ idea about _______. I agree with _______. Also, _______. While I can see why you believe this, I see it differently. In my opinion _______. That's a valid point, but I feel _______. I do agree with the part about _______ but _______.
Expressing Your Own Ideas	I believe that _______. In my opinion _______. I think that _______ because _______. My experience with _______ makes me think _______.

Discussion Techniques

There are so many techniques and protocols that provide options for students to participate effectively in discussions. Often, as teachers, we assign a protocol to students. In every group, for example, students participate in a Socratic seminar, a chalk talk, or concentric circles. Similarly, in a virtual class, we may group students and provide them with the protocol for their work in breakout rooms. Instead, consider providing a choice board to each group so they can review the purpose of the discussion and decide on the best format or protocol to work toward their goals. Table 4 is an example of a choice board where learners can choose which collaboration strategy would work best for their discussion. These discussions can be done in person or virtually, using breakout rooms.

Table 4: A Choice Board Where Learners Can Choose Their Collaboration Strategy

Discussion Techniques Choice Board	
Team Roles	Students work together, and each has a primary role within the team. Some examples of roles are: • Manager (to keep the team on task) • Reader (to read the question aloud) • Encourager (to make sure everyone participates) • Checker (to make sure everyone understands) • Writer (to record discussion)
Fishbowl	The group splits into Team 1 and Team 2. Team 1 engages in a discussion or collaborates on a problem-solving challenge. Team 2 listens, observes, and makes notes on Team 1's work. They focus their attention on the team dynamic and make sure they are prepared to discuss how well or poorly Team 1 worked together. Then, the teams switch.

Graffiti Team Time	Each person in the group poses an open-ended question and writes it on a piece of chart paper, a miniature white board, or a slide in a shared document. The team passes around the paper or rotates through a shared document, and each person brainstorms answers to the questions. Once everyone has contributed to each question, the group critiques/analyzes the responses.
Constructive Controversy	Groups of four are organized into pairs, who are assigned opposing sides of an issue. Each pair researches their assigned position, and the group discusses the issue with the goal of exposing as much information about the subject as possible. Pairs can then switch sides to assume the opposite position and continue the discussion.
Paraphrase Passport	This discussion structure requires each team member to listen actively to what is being shared by the other group members, so they can correctly paraphrase or restate the idea of the teammate who previously spoke. Once they've successfully paraphrased the previous point, then they can contribute their own idea.
Concentric Circles	The group forms two circles, one inside the other. Each student on the inside is paired with a student on the outside, and they face each other. The students discuss a question for a set amount of time, and then the inner circle rotates so the students have discussions with new partners.

Strategy #3: Student-Designed Asynchronous Online Discussions

In a blended learning environment, discussions may take place asynchronously online via text or video. This is an opportunity to allow students to craft their own discussion questions to engage their peers in academic conversations online. Just as in-person discussions require explicit instruction, scaffolds, and practice, writing a dynamic online discussion question is a bit of an art form. There are strategies students can employ to ensure that the discussion questions they are producing are more likely to engage all members of a group or the class. Figure 8 shows some tips you will want to share with students to ensure that their online discussion prompt yields high levels of participation.

Figure 8: Tips for Designing Dynamic Online Discussion Questions

Tip #1: Creative + Catchy Title

Tip #2: Layer your questions to achieve subtle differentiation for students at different levels. Ask the most academically rigorous question first. Follow this first question with two additional questions that allow students more entry points into the conversation.

Tip #3: Always include media in your question.

Tip #4: Include directions for student participation. Once they post their response to your question, what do they need to do? How many peers should they respond to?

Tip #1: Start with a catchy and creative title. In a text-based discussion inside of an LMS, the title is the first thing students see. Typically, students have to click the discussion title to expand it and see the actual discussion questions. That's why it is essential to begin with a title that is going to hook the students' attention and pique their interest. "Chapter 15 Discussion Question" won't cut it, but "The Danger of Mob Mentality" might!

Tip #2: Layer your questions to subtly differentiate. A class is composed of students with a wide range of skills, abilities, and language proficiencies, so you should avoid asking just a single question. This only allows one entry point into the conversation and may make it challenging for *all* students to participate in the discussion. Instead, encourage students to write three questions that move from more challenging to more accessible. They can combine different types of questions (e.g., analytical, compare/contrast, reflective) to provide their peers with options so they do not all have to answer the exact same question. Remind them to consider what words they are using and whether that vocabulary is going to be accessible for all students.

For example, an English teacher crafting questions to engage a diverse class of students in an online discussion about "The Danger of Mob Mentality" focusing on Chapter 15 in *To Kill a Mockingbird* could use the following questions to subtly differentiate:

- Why does being part of being a group diffuse, or lessen, the sense of individual responsibility people feel about their actions?
- Why do people act differently when part of a group or crowd compared to the way they act on their own?
- Have you ever felt peer pressure to act in a particular way because you were with a group of friends?

Tip #3: Always—always—include media. We are teaching a generation of visual students, who enjoy engaging with all types of media.

As students craft their discussion questions, they should think about media that will complement those questions. They should embed a photo, graphic, chart, video clip, etc. to pique their peers' interest and get them thinking about the topic more deeply.

Tip #4: Include guidelines for participation. Once the students have crafted their discussion questions, they should end with a clear statement about what their peers should do after they answer the question. How many classmates should they respond to? How long should those responses be? What strategies can they use to ensure that their replies to peers are substantive and meaningful?

For example, students could end their discussion questions with a statement like:

> Once you have responded to the discussion questions, read the other responses and reply thoughtfully to two other students, complimenting strong points made, building on ideas shared, offering another perspective, and/or asking specific questions.

Strategy #4: Self-Assess Discussions

Too often, there is a fear that if students create their own questions and choose their own format for discussion then all hell will break loose! We completely understand the importance of creating accountability for student discussions and think it's critical that groups set goals for discussions, reflect on those goals and the effectiveness of their discussion, and then assess their contributions as well as the overall quality of the conversation. This can be done by asking students to reflect on the discussion holistically, using a list of predetermined reflection questions, or by asking them to reflect on the effectiveness of their engagement in the conversation using a simple rubric, like the one in Figure 9. This tool can be used to

Figure 9: Small-Group Participation Rubric

Self-Assessment: Participation in Small-Group Discussion
1: Beginning • Limited to no participation in discussions. • Did not come to discussions prepared and/or did not support statements with evidence that reflected preparation. • Few attempts to ask questions or build on ideas shared.
2: Developing • Some participation in the discussion. • Limited attempts to support statements with evidence and examples that reflected preparation. • Some attempts to ask questions, build on ideas shared, or make connections.
3: Proficient • Consistent participation in the discussion. • Came to the discussion prepared. Drew on that preparation to support points. • Attempted to drive conversations forward by asking questions, building on ideas shared, and making connections. • Responded to diverse perspectives, summarized points, and made connections. • Made eye contact and spoke loud enough to be heard.
4: Mastery • Consistent participation in the discussion and invited quieter voices into the conversation. • Came to the discussion prepared. Explicitly drew on that preparation, providing evidence and examples to support points made. • Propelled conversation forward by posing and responding to questions that related to the current discussion. • Responded thoughtfully to diverse perspectives, summarized points of agreement and disagreement, and made new connections. • Made eye contact, listened actively, and spoke loud enough to be heard.
• Explain your self-assessment score. • What do you specifically want to improve on in future discussions?

prompt learners to reflect on a discussion and identify areas they need to focus on improving.

If you conclude a discussion with a reflective practice, you can provide a choice board, like the one in Figure 10, to provide students with numerous options for sharing reflections, including a traditional written response, poem, diary entry, video, audio recording, infographic, or sketchnotes.

Figure 10: Post-discussion Reflection Strategy Choice Board

Self-Assessment: Participation in Small-Group Discussion		
Write a summary of the Main Points	Write a Song or Poem	Create Sketchnotes
Record a Video	Make an Audio Recording	Design an Infographic
Make Connections with a Concept Map	Write a Journal Entry	

When students have an opportunity to stop and reflect at the end of the discussion, it can help them identify the main ideas shared, capture important connections they were able to make during the discussion, and cement their understanding of key concepts. A post-discussion reflection also creates space for students to think about their individual contributions to the discussion, consider the feedback they received from their peers, and set specific goals for themselves before the next discussion.

WRAP-UP

The traditional teacher-led IRF model has outlived its prime. We can make our workloads more sustainable and increase student engagement when we shift from teacher-led, whole-class discussion to student-led, small-group discussion. When we encourage students to formulate their questions, choose the format of the discussion and the roles they assume within their group, and assess their contributions and efficacy in collaborative teams, we are shifting the process of making meaning to students and fostering expert learning in the classroom. Facilitating these small groups in a station rotation model can scaffold these critical skills and provide you with opportunities to offer feedback while students build more independence, leading and interacting with their peers.

REFLECT AND DISCUSS

1. As you think about fostering discussions in your classroom, reflect on an unlearning process you have already gone through. Use the sentence frame, "I used to think ___________, then I thought ___________ but now I think ___________."
2. How can co-creating norms help to build student ownership of the culture and climate of student-led discussions?
3. How do your current discussion practices compare to the recommendations in this chapter, where students take ownership of the process, pathway, and pace of their discussions?

4. What additional supports and scaffolds might you make available to help students successfully engage in discussion in person and online?
5. When might you have students engage in online discussions versus asking them to engage in small-group in-class discussions? What are the advantages and challenges you associate with online versus in-person discussions?

PUTTING IT INTO PRACTICE

Choose one of the strategies outlined in this chapter to move toward more student-led learning in your classroom.

- Strategy #1: Co-create norms
- Strategy #2: Scaffolds for the win
- Strategy #3: Student-designed asynchronous online discussions
- Strategy #4: Self-assess discussions

Planning Template 2: Student-Led Discussions Lesson

Learning objective or desired result: • What would you like students to know, understand, or be able to do at the end of this discussion? • Which discussion skills would you like them to develop as a result of participating in this conversation?	
Grouping strategy: • How will you group students (e.g., mixed skill level, interest-based)?	

Discussion strategy:
• Select the discussion strategy you want to focus on.
  ○ Co-creating norms
  ○ Team roles
  ○ Fishbowl
  ○ Graffiti team time
  ○ Constructive controversy
  ○ Paraphrase passport
  ○ Concentric circles
  ○ Student-designed online discussions	

Outline the process and steps. Include information on the following: • What steps will students move through? • What supports and scaffolds will they need? • What mechanisms are embedded in the lesson to collect formative assessment data? • How will you encourage self-assessment and/or reflective practice?	

WORKFLOW SHIFT #3

From Reading as Solitary Endeavor to Reading for Connection

Women, Wine, and a Book Club

Catlin

My four closest girlfriends and I get together for dinner, wine, and conversation every couple of months. It requires a Herculean effort to coordinate our five schedules to meet up without children or partners. As we have navigated motherhood, marriages, divorces, and careers, we have come to treasure this time together. Yet, it can be challenging to prioritize these evenings in the face of life's many demands.

One night after dinner, the topic of books and what we were reading surfaced in the conversation. At the time, I was reading *The Guernsey Literary and Potato Peel Pie Society*, a novel by Mary Ann Shaffer and Annie Barrows. I talked animatedly about the story, and two of my girlfriends expressed interest in reading it. Without giving it much thought, I blurted out, "We should start a book club!"

A book club would give us an excuse to plan a monthly get-together while also providing an incentive to read, something we all wanted to do more of but often neglected in the day-to-day craziness of life. My girlfriends were on board, and our book club was born! We decided to take turns selecting a book and hosting the evening, which would involve dinner, drinks, and lots of talking. The host would develop or find discussion questions online to spark conversation about what we were reading.

Even though I had known these women for more than twenty years, some of their selections surprised me. We read dense historical nonfiction, "beach reads" light on substance and full of drama, self-help guides, true crime, and classic novels. I'll be honest. I only *really* enjoyed about every third book we read. I found the nonfiction texts dry and less compelling, and the self-help books often felt repetitive and not super relevant to my life. During the months when we read one of those texts, I felt like I was slogging through the mud trying to finish the book in time for our meeting. I was far less motivated to read when I didn't enjoy the genre or subject. In the months when we read a true crime or dystopian novel, I was all in! I could not put those books down and had no trouble finishing them. The experience helped me to appreciate how individual reading preferences can impact a person's desire to read.

Not only did we enjoy different types of books, but the way we engaged with those books varied as well. I would bounce between reading a hard copy and listening to the Audible version of a book when I had a busy month and knew I would not have time to read the whole thing curled in front of a fire at home. Having that audio version allowed me to listen in the car, on a plane, at the gym, or walking my dog. When I had time to read at home, I would pick up my book, find my spot, and continue reading. When I shared this with the group, one woman said, "That's a great idea! I struggle to stay focused when I read at home. I bet an audio recording would help." One of my other friends said her new favorite routine was getting up thirty minutes earlier to make tea and read before her family woke up and the chaos of getting kids ready for school started.

We also processed the reading differently. I made tons of scribbles and notes in the margins of my books, annotating like I did as an English major in college. One girlfriend drew symbols and arrows to track important ideas, characters, and connections. Another friend recorded notes on her phone, capturing moments of significance and questions she wanted to discuss. It was fascinating to see the variation in our approaches!

Even though I did not love every book we read, I did love talking about the reading with my friends. It allowed us to share personal stories, connections, and insights, which brought us closer together and often provided another perspective on the subject of the text. I thoroughly enjoyed the opportunity that our book club gave us to connect and share our ideas. I also appreciated what I learned about myself as a reader and how not one-size-fits-all reading is!

The Research and Reality: Redefining Literacy

In 2003, we were both hired as high school English teachers and had the same exact experience. On the first day of school, we were handed a photocopied list of district-approved texts and told we had to pick six of them. There were not enough copies of each book for multiple teachers to teach the same title simultaneously, so we had to submit our selections in the order we wanted to teach them, which was added to a book-rotation schedule. We both had exactly six weeks to usher a group of thirty-plus students through a text and return the books to the library for the next teacher on the schedule waiting for them.

This approach was problematic on several fronts. First, the small number of district-approved titles and physical copies meant we could not allow students to regularly select texts of interest. Instead, the entire class trudged through the same text at the same pace, despite the wide variety of reading abilities, language proficiencies, and reading preferences in our classrooms.

Second, students rarely enjoyed the opportunity to control the pace of their reading. Some texts were dense or lengthy and took students longer to get through than the six weeks allowed. We often found ourselves assigning more reading in a week than we would have liked in order to get students through the text in the time allotted. That caused students stress, anxiety, and frustration. If we wanted students to actually read the books, we had to dedicate significant class time to reading these texts together instead of engaging in conversations or developing and honing reading skills, like applying comprehension strategies and analyzing main ideas to understand how they developed in a text.

Finally, there were students in our high school English classes who were reading at a second- or third-grade level, and they could not access the information in these texts. Because the texts we read, at that point, were exclusively paperback books or photocopies of online articles (some of which had pages missing!), these students were shut out of the experience entirely.

Given the range of barriers that exist when students are asked to read traditional texts in a whole-group, lockstep lesson, it should not surprise anyone that so many students do not enjoy reading. If students do not have the opportunity to select texts that are interesting and accessible or to

> *If students do not have the opportunity to select texts that are interesting and accessible or to dictate the pace at which they read, they are less likely to find the experience pleasurable or rewarding. Yet reading to learn is a critical life skill our students need to continue learning long after they leave our classrooms.*

dictate the pace at which they read, they are less likely to find the experience pleasurable or rewarding. Yet reading to learn is a critical life skill our students need to continue learning long after they leave our classrooms.

So, how do we cultivate expert readers? How can we leverage UDL, blended learning, and technology to create flexible pathways where students have meaningful choices? We need to create reading workflows that allow for student agency, differentiation, or student control over the pace at which they read.

UDL was born because of the inaccessibility of printed text. According to the founders of the UDL framework, "When we were forming CAST in the 1980s, we envisioned the new technologies as learning tools that could be radically different from the medium of print. Because digital tools offered flexibility in how content was displayed and acted on, we believed that they could be powerful levers for students who most needed better leverage."[1] If students only have opportunities to obtain new information, rich vocabulary, and appreciate an author's craft through printed text, we exclude students who cannot yet decode at grade level, multilingual learners, and students who are visually impaired.

Reading is an exchange of views between the reader and the writer.[2] This exchange has to be both accessible and engaging; this requires flexibility and choice. A printed text isn't going to cut it for everyone. Those with reading challenges may need the text read aloud; those with limited vocabulary may need linked definitions or visuals; those with physical challenges may need to turn pages with a digital interface.[3] Voilà—digital technologies, like audiobooks and ebooks, provide these levers if we are flexible enough to allow them in our classrooms.

---

1 Meyer, Gordon, and Rose, *Universal Design for Learning*, 1.

2 Ibrahim Halil Yurdakal, "Investigation of the 4th Grade Primary School Students' Attitudes towards Reading in the Scope of Different Variables," *World Journal of Education* 9, no. 3 (June 25, 2019): 46.

3 Meyer, Gordon, and Rose, *Universal Design for Learning*.

Only about a third of students in the United States are reading at grade level, and another third cannot yet function at a basic level of literacy.[4] Piling inaccessible books on the laps of students who are not yet capable of reading independently has increased neither reading proficiency nor a love for reading, so it's time to put traditional practices and hard copies of whole-class novels to bed.

The Every Student Succeeds Act (ESSA) defines comprehensive literacy as instruction that includes multiple components. Two of those components are:

- uses strategies to enhance children's motivation to read and write and children's engagement in self-directed learning;
- incorporates the principles of universal design for learning[5]

Building student self-direction in literacy requires students to be expert learners and expert readers, both of which require self-awareness and reflection. An expert at learning, according to the UDL founders, is "someone who is continually growing and developing through introspection and guided feedback from other experts and peers. Key to expert learning is self-knowledge as a learner."[6] We want to offer the concept of "expert reader" through a UDL lens. In Table 5, the left column introduces the questions that expert learners consistently ask themselves. We have adapted these questions for readers.

Think about how you would answer the questions. Then consider offering the same questions to your students as you begin to shift from teacher-directed text instruction to building students as expert readers. Be sure to provide students with multiple means of expression as they share their answers. Could they write responses, record a video or a podcast, or answer in an infographic or sketch?

4 Joel R. Montgomery, "Using Audio Books to Improve Reading and Academic Performance" (working paper, 2009), files.eric.ed.gov/fulltext/ED505947.pdf .

5 Every Student Succeeds Act of 2015, Pub L. No. 114-95, Stat. 1802 (2015).

6 Meyer, Gordon, and Rose, *Universal Design for Learning*.

Table 5: Reflection Questions for Expert Learners and Expert Readers

Expert Learning	Expert Reading
What are my strengths and weaknesses?	What are my strengths and weaknesses as a reader?
What is the optimal setting for me to learn?	What environment best helps me to engage deeply with the text I am reading?
Which tools amplify my abilities and support my areas of weakness?	What tools can I use when I am reading to help me make sense of vocabulary I don't know or build background knowledge I don't have yet?
How do I best learn from peers?	How can I discuss and collaborate with peers after shared reading of a text to increase my own comprehension and appreciation of the text?
How can I support myself when I feel anxious about an upcoming challenge?	What are the best strategies for helping me to build reading stamina?
How can I be open to unlearning mistaken or outdated understandings and building new ones?	How can I be open-minded to new ideas and ways of thinking when I am reading?
How can I learn from my mistakes?	What strategies can I use to increase my fluency and comprehension when I am reading?

Figure 11: Expert Reader Reflection Sheet

Expert Readers Regularly Reflect	
It's time to reflect! Reflection is an important part of the learning process. It helps us to understand ourselves as learners—our strengths, weaknesses, and needs. Directions: Take a few minutes to reflect on the following questions. You can choose to write your thoughts down or record a video or audio track answering each of these questions. If you choose to record a video or audio track, include the link to your recording on this document.	
Expert Reader Reflection Sheet	
What are my strengths and weaknesses as a reader?	
What environment best helps me to engage deeply in the text I am reading?	
What tools can I use when I am reading to help me make sense of vocabulary I don't know or background information I don't have?	
How can I discuss and collaborate with peers after shared reading of a text to increase my own comprehension and appreciation of the text?	
What are the best strategies for helping me to build reading stamina?	
How can I be open-minded to new ideas and ways of thinking when I am reading?	
What strategies can I use to increase my fluency and comprehension when I am reading?	

Helping students understand their reading lives is critical to developing their self-awareness and making responsible decisions about their learning experience. As we use blended learning models to provide students with more flexibility in path, pace, and place, self-awareness and self-regulation are essential to their success.

So, how do you get started shifting the workflow from the hard copy of the whole-class novel? We share five strategies here. All of the strategies can be used with or to supplement an adopted curriculum. We recognize that not every teacher has the autonomy to choose their curriculum materials. We also know that the lessons in many adopted curricula are written for a whole-group lesson that's teacher-led and teacher-paced, so these strategies may require that you think creatively about how you use an adopted curriculum. Regardless of your program, grade level, or content area, you can use required reading programs or textbooks while shifting ownership to students.

Strategy #1: If You Have a Shared Text, Make It Accessible

Although we advocate for students to choose their texts most of the time, this does not mean that students choose their texts all the time. We know that primary source documents can't be replicated and that sometimes a text is so powerful we want to share an excerpt of it with the entire class. We also recognize that some of you will have a curriculum where students are required to read specific texts. When you are universally designing your classroom and using blended learning models to change your reading workflow, it doesn't mean that you can't assign a text. Rather, universally designed blended learning strives to balance high-quality, diverse texts shared in accessible formats with texts that students choose themselves, in formats that are most accessible to them. In addition to prioritizing their agency, universally designed blended learning provides students with opportunities to control the pace of their progress through a text.

> *Universally designed blended learning strives to balance high-quality, diverse texts shared in accessible formats with texts that students choose themselves, in formats that are most accessible to them.*

As we both advocate, all students should have access to grade-level texts regardless of their reading level. Even if books are frustrating for students, researchers advise that hearing challenging texts aloud will help students become familiar with difficult vocabulary.[7] Many educators understand that audiobooks are necessary for students who face barriers to reading traditional text, but they struggle with providing more accessible options to *all* learners. As UDL practitioners, we have to remember that what is necessary for some students is a good option to provide to all learners.

We sometimes hear that audiobooks should not be provided for students who have strong reading comprehension skills because it is cheating or it will make them "lazy." This is not supported by research. *Time* magazine featured an article, "Are Audiobooks as Good for You as Reading? Here's What Experts Say," which begins with:

> "I was a fan of audiobooks, but I always viewed them as cheating," says Beth Rogowsky, an associate professor of education at Bloomsburg University of Pennsylvania.
>
> For a 2016 study, Rogowsky put her assumptions to the test. One group in her study listened to sections of *Unbroken*, a nonfiction book about World War II by Laura Hillenbrand, while a second group read the same parts

7 Roselmina Indrisano and Jeanne S. Chall, "Literacy Development," *Journal of Education* 177, no. 1 (January 1995): 63–83.

> on an e-reader. She included a third group that both read and listened at the same time. Afterward, everyone took a quiz designed to measure how well they had absorbed the material. "We found no significant differences in comprehension between reading, listening, or reading and listening simultaneously," Rogowsky says.[8]

The article goes on to caution that audiobooks can create barriers to reading comprehension if readers try to multitask. We are both guilty of that sometimes! I mean, how cool is it to listen to a book club selection while preparing dinner? When the option is available, we can remind our students about the purpose for reading and that "if you're trying to learn while doing two things, you're not going to learn as well."[9]

Some of you may not have audio versions of texts readily available, but there are still ways to ensure that students have opportunities to listen to texts. You can record an audio file of yourself or a student reading the text, or you can provide options for students to read silently or work with a partner who reads the text aloud.

Once students can perceive text, visually or through listening, it's also important that any shared reading is scaffolded for all learners. Understanding evidence-based scaffolding strategies for different literacy domains will ensure that all students have access to and opportunities to read and respond to rich, rigorous grade-level texts. Review the challenges and solutions presented in Table 6 and consider which scaffolds and supports you proactively provide to all learners. You may want to note scaffolds that you are not yet incorporating into your practice. As a next step, reflect on your strategies and set goals for putting more inclusive practices into action.

---

8 Markham Heid, "Are Audiobooks as Good for You as Reading? Here's What Experts Say," *Time*, September 6, 2018, time.com/5388681/audiobooks-reading-books/.

9 Ibid.

Table 6: Barriers to Reading, Scaffolds, and Supports

Overcoming Barriers #1: Independently Reading a Text and Answering Comprehension Questions
Before Reading: • Start with an essential guiding question to be previewed before reading that states the purpose for reading. • Include pictures or images that align with the text. • Teach a set of vocabulary words, intentionally using a variety of instructional activities. • Provide summaries of the text to build background information before reading or listening to the text, if helpful. During Reading: • In addition to the text, provide a read-aloud via peer model, teacher, an audio version, or text-to-speech. • Provide translations for students to build background information in L1 before reading/listening to the text.

Overcoming Barriers #2: Writing in Response to Text
• Provide sentence or paragraph frames so students can write about what they read. • Provide pictures or a word bank to go along with the sentence frames. • Use language-based supports like graphic organizers to provide students the support they need. • Provide samples of writing artifacts that students can model their writing after. • Provide options for writing by hand, typing, or speech-to-text. • Use small groups or pairs to provide opportunities for students to work and talk together on varied aspects of writing in response to text.

Overcoming Barriers #3: Discussing Learning with Peers

- Reflect, as a class, on videos of peer conversations for an effective model.
- Give students time to write or draw quietly to prepare for the discussion.
- Provide sentence starters so all students can participate in focused discussion.
- Co-create or use protocols to ensure that all learners have opportunities to converse with classmates and contribute to conversations.

Strategy #2: Allow Students to Select Texts

The one-size-fits-all approach to text selection was a necessity when teachers were limited to texts in a book room; however, technology and online resources are making it possible for educators to rethink this traditional approach. We can often allow students to select their own texts as they work toward "firm goals" as a stand-alone activity or to supplement the curriculum. This helps all students have access to "mirrors, windows, and sliding glass doors," as Rudine Sims Bishop calls them in a seminal article that helped to highlight the power of literature to celebrate student identity while also building empathy and diversity.[10] Given the incredible variability and diversity of our students, it is critical that we allow them to choose texts written by people who share their identity and characters who speak to their lived experiences. Regardless of the subject you teach, you can encourage students to find stories of characters or real people who have succeeded in your content area. Encourage students to get curious and bring in resources and find writers that speak to their lived experiences.

This freedom to provide students with meaningful choices in relation to reading should be exciting, but many teachers are still not

10 Rudine Sims Bishop, "Windows, Mirrors, and Sliding Glass Doors," *Perspectives: Choosing and Using Books in the Classroom* 6, no. 3 (1990).

sure how to approach teaching when students are reading different texts. They are used to assigning a single reading assignment that is often paired with comprehension questions for all students to complete, like the questions provided at the end of textbook chapters and in novel studies. This traditional approach to reading and assessing comprehension is unlikely to inspire a lifelong love of reading, and it yields stacks of work (both physical and digital) that teachers feel pressure to read and assess. Choice in reading is absolutely necessary to build reading proficiency and reading joy. Research argues that if students become enthusiastic readers of *any* type of reading, they will progress enormously.[11] Now, some of you are reading this and thinking, "It's not my job to instill a love of literacy. That is the English teacher's responsibility." Hear us out. Content-area literacy requires students to read, write, speak, and listen in every subject, and providing a balance of content-specific texts, multimedia, and narratives helps students appreciate how each subject is both scientific and artistic. Every single one of our subjects was built by people. Learning more about the pioneers in our field, the lives they lived, the places they explored, and the work they were passionate about can instill joy in our learners.

If students have a choice about what text they read, we have to reimagine our approach to having them engage with a text and demonstrate their comprehension. Instead of asking all students to answer the exact same questions, we must provide them with choices about how they a) engage with their chosen texts and b) demonstrate their comprehension of those texts as they work toward grade-level standards.

Imagine you have given students four biographies, informational texts, or short stories to preview and choose from. Perhaps

11 S. D. Krashen, "Free Voluntary Reading: Still a Very Good Idea," in *Explorations in Language Acquisition and Use* by S. D. Krashen (Portsmouth, NH: Heinemann, 2003), 15–29.

you present those choices in the form of a digital exit ticket (as pictured in Figure 12) at the end of class.

Content area literacy requires students to read, write, speak, and listen in every subject, and providing a balance of content-specific texts, multimedia, and narratives help students appreciate how each subject is both scientific and artistic.

When students arrive for the next class, you put them in groups with other students who selected the same text, as in Figure 13. Not only does this approach give students the agency to choose a text of interest, but it provides peer support and social engagement as they read.

Before the groups begin reading, you can provide them with a few strategies in the form of a collaborative active-reading choice board, as pictured in Figure 14. Some group members may prefer a more traditional approach, like capturing annotations in a collaborative digital document. Some group members may enjoy a more artistic approach and want to sketch images and capture "golden lines" as they read. Others may prefer a discussion-based approach to engage with the ideas presented in a text. Ideally, the group should spend a few minutes exploring and discussing the different strategies. They can then identify the reading activity they are most interested in and create pairings or smaller groupings based on the strategy they have selected from the choice board.

Figure 12: Exit Ticket—Reading to Learn about Famous People in Math

Famous people in the field of math: Who do you want to read about?

Next class we will be learning about people who had an impact on the field of math. Who would you like to read about?

* Required

Name *

Your answer

Class Period *

- [ ] Period1
- [ ] Period 3
- [ ] Period 5

Select the person you want to learn more about. *

- ◯ Elbert Frank Cox–American professor–first African-American to receive a PhD in Mathematics
- ◯ Alan Turing–British mathematician–codebreaker and the father of computer science
- ◯ Emmy Noether–German mathematician–known for her contributions to abstract algebra
- ◯ William Playfair–Scottish engineer–the founder of graphical statistics

Submit

Clear form

Figure 13: Interest-Based Reading Groups in Math

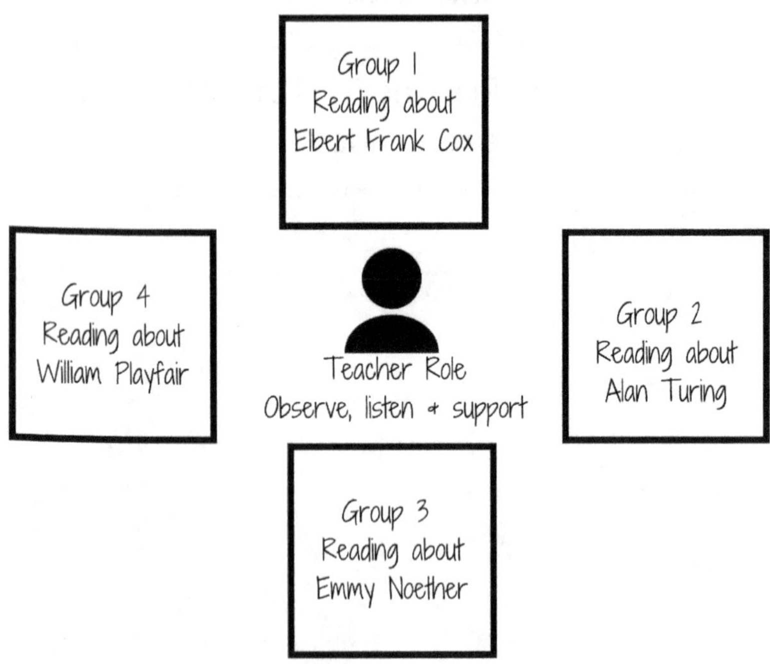

Regardless of the strategy they use, your workload will be significantly reduced when students create a shared product. And that shared product does *not* need to be formally assessed. Instead, you an spend your time moving around the room or bouncing into and of breakout rooms to listen, observe, and offer support. The sim- of watching and listening can provide invaluable formative t data that can help you identify which groups or group comprehending the reading and which may be strug- or group member is struggling with their selected that individual or group to provide support by ngaging the group in discussion, and clarifying

Figure 14: Collaborative Active-Reading Activities Choice Board

Collaborative Active-Reading Activities Choice Board
Collaborative Annotations on a Shared Google Document • Make a copy of the annotation template in Google Classroom and share it with the members of your group. • Each group member should select a color font to type in. • Capture your thoughts (e.g., big ideas, connections, questions) on your collaborative document as you read. 
Group Sketchnotes & Golden Lines • Lay down a big piece of butcher paper or poster paper in the center of your group. • As you read, sketch objects and images that represent the big ideas or events from the text. • Use arrows and other symbols to show the connections between the ideas and events. 

Read, Pause, Discuss, Repeat
• Decide how often your group will pause in the text to discuss the reading.
• Once you've decided on your pausing points, read silently and note any questions you want to discuss when you arrive at:
  ○ Main ideas
  ○ Important people
  ○ Key issues

Strategy #3: Co-creating Text Sets

The Literacy Design Collaborative defines texts in the twenty-first century as a range of artifacts, including print, visual, and multimedia types.[12] Text sets are collections of texts focused on specific topics to support all learners in building background knowledge and vocabulary. Oftentimes, a "short profound text" is used as an anchor text and is paired with other short profound texts, including multimedia and visual texts like maps, artworks, data, video, and timelines.

As the teacher, you may feel pressure to create the text sets yourself, but in a universally designed blended learning environment, you have an incredible opportunity to co-create text sets with students. When you curate a text set with students, you reduce your workload and ensure that texts are relevant, authentic, and meaningful to the students you serve. First, introduce the short profound text that will anchor the instruction (i.e., a chapter in your textbook, short story, painting, composition, or primary-source document), and then encourage students to form teams that will add supplements to the text set. One group of students could look for visual images that connect to the standard or content under study, while another group explores relevant podcasts, TED Talks, or digital media. You may be concerned that students will not find relevant and authentic texts. If that is the case, you can minimize that barrier by co-creating a rubric for selection or you can share a list of reputable websites that students can explore to find paired texts.

As an example, the *New York Times* shares the power of digital images in its weekly feature "What's Going On in This Picture?"[13] Each day, they share a picture from the *NYT* archives that requires

12 Literacy Design Collaborative, "LDC," LDC Template Task Collection 2.0, 2013, ccsoh.us/cms/lib/OH01913306/Centricity/Domain/207/Rubrics%20LDC%202.0.pdf.

13 "What's Going On in This Picture?," *New York Times*, accessed March 5, 2022, nytimes.com/column/learning-whats-going-on-in-this-picture.

viewers to become detectives to determine what is going on. They encourage the following questions:

- What's going on in this picture?
- What do you see that makes you say that?
- What more can you find?[14]

The editors note, "Closely reading any text, whether written or visual, requires that students proceed more slowly and methodically, noticing details, making connections and asking questions. This takes practice. But it certainly helps when students want to read the text." They go on to say, "Indeed, practicing visual thinking skills with these images can be fun and a quick activity, but it can also hone important skills that transfer to other texts."[15] Empowering your visual team to review the archive of photos may be a great activity to build ownership of the text set while also helping students make connections and develop research and collaboration skills.

If you teach younger students, you may want to ask a parent helper, an honors society student at the high school, or pre-service teachers at a local university to help create authentic and culturally responsive text sets. In math and science class, you can encourage students to find case studies, research articles, or authentic data sets. Students can find audio files, videos of performances, or interesting biographies of musicians in music class. In PE, students can peruse "People Are Awesome" videos online to find examples of humans accomplishing what looks impossible with their bodies through physical fitness. Think about the "text" that students need to explore and empower students to add depth and richness by pairing it with additional artifacts to build background, make connections, and leverage digital media.

---

14 Ibid.

15 Michael Gonchar, "10 Intriguing Photographs to Teach Close Reading and Visual Thinking Skills," The Learning Network, accessed March 8, 2022, learning.blogs.nytimes.com/2015/02/27/10-intriguing-photographs-to-teach-close-reading-and-visual-thinking-skills/.

During a complex text lesson, instruction may be scaffolded, but it is critical that the text at the center of instruction is at or above grade level. The primary quantitative leveling tool used to determine "grade level" text is Lexile. Texts also have qualitative complexity. If you are looking for complex text, there are a few places you can access high-quality texts for free.

- CommonLit has a library of high-quality grade-level texts paired with additional texts and multimedia in text sets.
- Appendix B of the Common Core provides exemplars ("short profound texts") for each grade that have grade-level complexity.
- The Smithsonian Tween Tribune has a collection of articles written at various Lexile levels.
- Readworks offers content in all subject areas for free.
- The Library of Congress has free primary sources you can search by recommended grade level (grades 3–12).
- The *New York Times* has a "Text to Text" feature that pairs a high-quality, well-known text with a *NYT* article. It's a great place to find paired text for high school readers.

Figure 15 is an example you can use as a model to prepare universally designed, culturally responsive text sets. We recommend building a playlist like this for students to closely read an anchor text and choose at least one text from each format, checking in with the teacher as they work through the text set at their own pace.

Figure 15: Building a Playlist

Paths	Options/Choices
Read anchor text. As you read or listen, focus your attention on the setting and how winter impacts the speaker of the poem.	Read or listen to "Dust of Snow" by Robert Frost. As you are reading, draw the setting you are imagining or find an image online that matches what you imagine.
Video exploration	Choose one of the following videos to learn more about snow. • "How Many Icicles Are There" from PBS Learning Media • "Surviving Winter" from PBS Learning Media
YOUR TURN Choose any place in the world and explore the weather in the winter in that location.	Compare/contrast the setting in "Dust of Snow" and the weather in the location you chose in the month of December. You may want to look at the average daily weather, watch weather reports, or look at snow accumulation if it gets cold enough. You can create a Venn diagram, write, or capture your comparison in a video or audio recording.
Check in with me! STOP	When you check in, be prepared to share how the setting in "Dust of Snow" and winter impact the author of the poem and how that is different from the way others are impacted by the winter.

YOUR TURN Read paired text.	Find a nonfiction article about the impact of a winter storm by researching more about one of the winter storms below. As you explore, consider the impact the storm had on people and their way of life. • The Blizzard of 1888—Northeastern United States • The Storm of the Century—Eastern United States, 1993 • Lhunze County, Tibet, 2008 • The Iran Blizzard of 1972, Iran and Azerbaijan
YOUR TURN Explore visual images.	Imagine you are opening up an art gallery and you want to feature art that portrays winter. Find at least two pieces of art (paintings, sculptures, dances, etc.) and note the impact of winter on the artist. You may want to take notes to prepare for your check-in with me, where you will share your analysis.
Check in with me! STOP	Share the art you explored and your analysis of how the artist was impacted by winter.
Assessment	How does winter impact people? Cite examples from the text set, your own experience, and other literature, art, or history in your answer. You can write or record your answer.

Strategy #4: Shift Control over the Pace of Reading to Students

Learner variability demands that we design with the intention of removing barriers and allowing students to complete tasks at a pace and on a path that works for them.

Like most teachers, we started our careers locating a single text we wanted to use, checking out books or making photocopies of said text, and guiding a whole-group reading of that text. However, we know that a teacher-paced whole-group approach to reading isn't effective for the majority of students. This one-size-fits-all approach traps the teacher at the front of the room and ultimately puts pressure on them to do most of the work by asking the class questions or highlighting important information.

This teacher-led whole-group model does not afford the teacher the time or space to meet the reading needs of individuals or small groups of students. We know that different students will struggle with different aspects of a text and will benefit from a variety of scaffolds and support. That's where universally designed blended learning can help! Blended learning models give students the time and space to move through a text at their own pace without feeling pressure to "keep up" with the rest of the class. They can look up unfamiliar vocabulary, re-read a section that was confusing, or pause to reflect on a powerful statement or quote. Blended learning models can also free the teacher to work alongside students as they read to support their progress through a text. That support might take the form of a conversation about the text, additional reading scaffolds (e.g., a graphic organizer), or more accessible mediums like audio versions of text or translations.

If you want all students to read the same text, using blended learning models gives students more autonomy and agency. Blended learning shifts control over the pace and, at times, the path of the learning to students, which has a positive impact on the students' ability to construct meaning and develop conceptual understanding.[16]

A playlist, like the one pictured in Figure 16, presents a sequence of learning activities for students to self-pace through. This playlist can be customized for a specific text or used to engage students who have selected a text of interest to read. The playlist is designed to help students develop specific reading skills, like identifying the main point, reading actively, and defining unfamiliar vocabulary. These are critical skills for students in every subject area to practice and hone. Given choice of topic or method, the right scaffolds, and time, all students will be able to read to learn—not just those who were strong readers from the start.

Although a playlist takes time to create, the return on that investment is substantial. During class, while students self-pace through the reading and work on the learning activities in the playlist, you can use your time to pull individual or small groups of students for personalized instruction and support. This time gives you the opportunity to connect with learners, collect formative assessment data, and make modifications to their playlists to ensure they continue making progress and developing as readers.

16 Wahyu Setyaningrum, "Blended Learning: Does It Help Students in Understanding Mathematical Concepts?," *Jurnal Riset Pendidikan Matematika* 5, no. 2 (November 22, 2018): 244–53.

Figure 16: Reading Mini-playlist

Reading Strategies Choice Board	
Directions	Your Work
Reflection: • Why did you select this text (e.g., title, cover, genre, topic)? • What do you already know about this topic? • What are you hoping to learn?	[Insert your text or a link]
Active Reading: • Would you rather: 1) annotate OR 2) draw sketchnotes as you read?	[Insert images of your annotations or sketchnotes]
Main Idea: • Identify the main idea in the text you are reading. • Clearly state the main idea and provide three details from the text that help to develop this main idea.	[Insert your text or a link]
Make Connections • How does what you learned reading this text connect with your prior knowledge? • How is this reading developing your understanding of this topic or extending your thinking? • What are you wondering as you read?	[Insert a photo of your concept map, your text, or a link to your audio recording]

<table>
<tr>
<td>Vocabulary Development:
• Select five new vocabulary words from your text that you want to spend time working with.
• Look up each word in the dictionary or online.
• Add the word and definition to your notes.
• Choose an activity from the vocabulary attainment choice board to complete with your chosen words.</td>
<td></td>
</tr>
<tr>
<td>Summary:
• Provide a summary of the text in your own words.</td>
<td>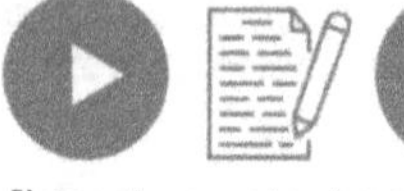
[Insert your text or a link]</td>
</tr>
</table>

Strategy #5: Encourage Students to Identify Reading Skills *They* Want to Focus On

Different students have different needs and require more or less time to develop critical skills, yet many classrooms are set up to provide all students with the exact same instruction and practice. If students are asked to do practice they do not need, they can become frustrated, bored, and disillusioned. Students who need additional instruction, scaffolding, and practice may not get it in a whole-group lesson. As a result, they may feel behind, lost, or uncertain of their skills and abilities. Just as the act of reading words on a page or screen takes students different amounts of time, students will need more or less time, practice, and support with reading strategies to become proficient at employing them as they read. For some students, asking and answering questions about the text may feel natural, while making inferences about a text based on the information presented may be a more daunting task. Students will benefit from differentiated instruction, interactive modeling sessions, and guided practice when first introduced to a reading strategy. Then they will need opportunities to practice skills, and some students will need additional time with the teacher.

A choice board, like the one pictured in Figure 17, gives students the agency to decide what reading strategy *they* want to focus on when engaging with a text. We know that teachers worry students may select an "easier" strategy or always choose the same strategy; however, if cultivating expert readers is our objective, students need opportunities to make these decisions. If you want to understand their choices and encourage metacognitive skill building, you can ask them to include an explanation about why they selected a specific reading strategy. Alternatively, you could ask them to complete a simple before-and-after self-assessment to encourage them to think critically about how a specific reading skill is developing with practice. We should not limit student agency because we are afraid of what students might decide when given choices. Instead, we should think about how we encourage students to think about why they are making certain choices and what impact those choices are having on their skill sets.

Figure 17: Reading Strategies Choice Board

<table>
<tr><th colspan="2">Reading Strategies Choice Board</th></tr>
<tr><td colspan="2">Select a reading strategy you want to practice as you read this text. As you annotate the text (offline or online), please document your thinking as you work on applying the reading strategy you selected.</td></tr>
<tr><td>Make Predictions
Stop regularly to think about what you have learned and use that information to predict what you think will happen in the text.</td><td>Asking and Answering Questions
Be a curious reader.
Stop frequently to ask questions—who, what, when, where, how, and why. Then pause when you can answer one of your questions.</td></tr>
</table>

Make Inferences

Pause after each paragraph or section of text and think about the information you've gathered. What conclusions or inferences can you make about people, events, and places based on that information?

Summarize the Text

After each section of the text, and again at the end, pause to think about the most important points. Write a summary presenting the main idea[s] in your own words.

Make Connections

As you read, make connections between:

- the different ideas presented
- the characters/people, events, places, and your own life experience
- the text and things you've learned in other classes

Use Context Clues to Define Unfamiliar Words

Stop when you encounter an unfamiliar word. Re-read the sentence carefully. What can you learn about the unknown word from the context clues? What do you think the word means based on how it is used?

Visualize and Draw

As you read, create pictures in your mind of characters, events, and scenes. Use the text's sensory details to bring these mental images to life. Stop periodically and draw what you see in your mind.

Identifying Explicit vs. Implicit Meaning

Stop after each paragraph and make a list of information that is explicitly (or directly) stated in the text. Then make a list of what is suggested (though not directly stated). What do you know without having to draw any conclusions? What is suggested or implied?

Use Your Prior Knowledge

As you read, think about your life experiences. How can your prior knowledge and past experiences help you understand the text (e.g., characters, situations, feelings, motivations, themes)?

If the class is reading a text—individually, in pairs, or in small groups—and focusing on a specific reading strategy or learning activity from a collection of options on a choice board, the teacher can use their time to facilitate an "optional skill station." This does just what the name suggests. The teacher will set up a stand-alone station and provide additional instruction, support, guided practice, and real-time feedback designed to help students struggling with a particular skill to develop their proficiency. The optional nature of this station gives students the agency to decide whether they think it will meet their specific needs. Does it target a skill they are struggling with? If so, they can join the station and complete the assignment with peer and teacher support. If not, they can focus on another skill that they need practice applying.

Before students begin the choice board assignment, let them know that you will be running an optional skill station or multiple skill stations targeting specific reading strategies. You can use formative assessment data to identify the reading strategies that multiple students are struggling with and to facilitate skill stations dedicated to providing students with additional instruction, practice, and support. For example, if students are struggling to summarize scientific articles or make inferences while reading primary-source documents, you can guide a small group through an I do–We do–Groups do–You do progression designed to help them develop confidence in their ability to employ this strategy. The small-group dynamic makes it easier to identify the gaps and misconceptions and then make the necessary adjustments to meet that group's needs.

The "optional" nature of this approach to providing additional instruction and support may cause some teachers to ask, "But what if I know students need more instruction or guided practice with a particular reading skill?" We understand the concern and know teachers have to make these strategies work for them and their students. So, if the data indicates specific students need more instruction in an area, then you can make a skill station a "must do" for some students and a "may do" for others. However, the goal should be for us to help learners develop a strong understanding of themselves, their skills, and their needs so they can decide if spending time at an optional skill station is the best use of their time in class.

WRAP-UP

Traditional approaches to reading may present a myriad of barriers for learners. Students may not enjoy the type of text they are asked to read. They may not have the vocabulary or background knowledge to understand the text. They may need more time to get through a particular text. All of these factors and more—interest, reading skills, prior knowledge, language proficiency, pacing—can make it challenging for students to access a shared text. However, technology and blended learning models provide more flexible pathways. Instead of moving lockstep through a single text as a class, teachers can put UDL into practice using blended learning models that prioritize student agency and autonomy, offer teachers more opportunities to consistently and effectively differentiate instruction and support, and allow learners more control over the pace of their reading.

REFLECT AND DISCUSS

1. Take a moment to reflect on the reading tasks you typically assign. What types of texts do your students read? How do you assess their understanding of those texts? Does this workflow require significant time and energy on your part?
2. What potential barriers exist that might make it challenging for all students to engage with the reading or complete the assigned reading task? What are some specific adjustments you might make to increase accessibility?
3. How often do you use digital texts versus print texts? What online resources are available to you that you can utilize to give

students more control over their experience (e.g., changing text size, offering access to an audio recording)? If you do not have resources like audio recordings available, do you have a teaching assistant or students who could record an audio track of texts you want to use?

4. What are the biggest challenges you associate with teaching students how to read subject-specific texts? How can the strategies presented in this chapter help you to mitigate or eliminate those challenges?
5. Review Table 5, which has the questions for expert readers to reflect on. Take a few minutes to answer these questions. Did any of your answers surprise you? Are there any questions you would add to this list? What options might you give your students for capturing and sharing their reflections?
6. Review Table 6 on the challenges presented by reading and some solutions for addressing those challenges. Which challenge do you observe most frequently when working with students? What are your thoughts on the proposed solutions? What are you currently doing? What might you try that you have not done before?

PUTTING IT INTO PRACTICE

Select one of the five strategies presented in this chapter that resonated most with you.

- Strategy #1: If you have a shared text, make it accessible
- Strategy #2: Allow students to select texts
- Strategy #3: Co-creating text sets
- Strategy #4: Shift control over the pace of reading to students
- Strategy #5: Encourage students to identify reading skills *they* want to focus on

Design a learning experience for your students that will shift the workflow from a teacher-centered, whole-group approach to a student-centered experience. As you work to design this universally designed blended learning experience, think about where students can enjoy more control over the time, place, pace, and path of their learning. Consider the barriers that might exist in the lesson and work to meet them with supports, scaffolds, and meaningful choice. Think about your role in the lesson. How will you use your time to more effectively meet your students' needs?

Once you've drafted a lesson that employs one of these strategies, share it with an audience for feedback—send it to a colleague, share it in a department meeting, write a blog, or record a video or podcast.

Planning Template 3: Reading for Connection Lesson

Learning objective or desired result: • What would you like students to know, understand, or be able to do at the end of this reading? • Which specific reading skills or comprehension strategies would you like students to develop as a result of participating in this activity?	
Grouping strategy: • How will you group students (e.g., mixed skill level, interest-based)? • Will you invite students to decide if they want to work alone, with a partner, or as part of a group?	
Select the reading strategy you want to use: • Making shared texts accessible • Allowing students to select texts • Co-creating text sets • Shifting control over the pace to learners • Encouraging students to identify the reading skills they want to focus on	

Where will you find texts? Do these texts have features, like audio recordings, that will make them more accessible for readers at different levels?	
What blended learning model or strategy will you use to shift control to students? • Station rotation model • Playlist model • Choice boards	
Take time to consider the following questions: • What blended learning model will you use to give students more control over the time, place, pace, or path of their learning? • How will you use your time during the lesson to maximize your impact? • What formative assessment data will you collect to measure student understanding and comprehension? • How will you ensure students have flexible pathways? Where can you provide meaningful choices to remove barriers?	

WORKFLOW SHIFT #4

From an Audience of One to an Authentic Audience

Taking the TED Stage

Catlin

In 2014, I was invited to the TED Conference in Vancouver. TED has recently started TED-Ed, their youth and education initiative, and they brought together a collection of educators to provide feedback on their new product for students. While in Vancouver, I watched several TED Talks, including Sting's talk about how he'd faced writer's block and found inspiration again. As I watched a parade of talented and inspiring speakers take the TED stage to share their passions and stories, I thought, "I want my students to do this!"

I volunteered to pilot the TED-Ed Club curriculum. It was designed to walk students through the process of identifying a topic or issue they were passionate about and crafting a dynamic talk. I was giddy at the prospect of my students delivering TED-style talks. I returned to my classroom and excitedly announced, "You all are going to give TED Talks!" They stared back at me, mouths agape. It was clear they did *not* share my enthusiasm for the idea.

After an awkward silence, one student finally said, "Who is going to want to watch our TED Talks?" I remember the sinking sensation in my stomach. These kids didn't believe they had anything of value to say. I was crestfallen. As their teacher, it was my job to help them find their voices and use them. If they didn't believe their voices and ideas were valuable, what had we been doing in this classroom all year?

Despite their obvious reluctance, I plowed on as any good teacher must do. We began working through the TED-Ed Club curriculum. Students selected topics of interest and issues about which they were passionate. They conducted research and interviews to learn more about their chosen subjects. As students worked on their talks, the atmosphere in my classroom shifted from trepidation and skepticism to enthusiasm and excitement.

I booked the theater on campus for the event, invited families to attend, and coordinated with the film teacher to have a senior record the talks. As the day approached, students requested time to rehearse with peers. They *wanted* feedback to improve, and they invested significant time preparing to deliver their talks. I had never seen students this engaged in a project. Presenting for an audience and knowing their talks would be recorded created an incentive to do their best work.

I sat in the audience, beaming with pride as I watched my students deliver their talks. They covered a range of topics, from reclaiming the word "feminism" to the need for more female comic book characters to embracing the chaos of life. My students were poised, knowledgeable, and enthusiastic. I was blown away.

My students uploaded their talks to their YouTube channels, and I passed a collection of talks to the TED-Ed team. Flash forward a few months, and I got an unexpected phone call from the folks at TED. They asked me to put them in touch with Anna, one of my students. They were so impressed by her talk on embracing chaos that they flew her and her father from Northern California to New York City to deliver her talk on the TED stage! She was stunned to receive the invitation. Despite the pressure of delivering it on such a prestigious stage, she nailed her talk. While in New York, Anna fell in love with the city and decided to attend NYU for college. That one project profoundly impacted the trajectory of her life.

After witnessing the impact of an authentic audience on both student motivation and the quality of their work, I believe the products our students create must be seen. Not just by us, their teachers, but by an actual audience. After my experience with the TED Talks, if I asked students to create something, I was also thinking about who the audience for that work would be. Would we do a gallery walk as a class, host an exhibition for family and friends, invite experts or community members to serve on a panel, or post their work to YouTube or their digital notebooks? I wanted to get as many eyes on student work as possible. That's how we shift their perspective on the value of the work they do so that instead of wanting their work to be "good enough," they want it to be excellent.

As I reflect on this moment in my career through the lens of UDL and blended learning, I recognize that delivering a TED Talk was likely not the best way for *all* of my students to share their passions with the world. Yes, some of my students thrived and enjoyed the experience. However, other students may have preferred to record their talks, create an animated film, design an infographic, write an article, or construct a model to share their ideas with the world. At that point in my career, I was not consistently providing flexible pathways and meaningful choices to ensure learning experiences were inclusive and equitable. If I were to do this project with students again, I would offer multiple ways for sharing ideas with an authentic audience to ensure that the endeavor felt relevant and accessible.

The Research and Reality: Elevating the Fresh and the Fearless

Grant Wiggins was a coauthor of *Understanding by Design*, a framework for curriculum design often referred to as "backward design." In an article in *English Journal*, Wiggins shared the importance of ensuring that student assessments have an authentic audience. Or rather, he lambasted assessments that do not have an authentic audience. He discusses that often the purpose of an assessment is simply to please the teacher. The article has a line that's pure gold: "Since most rubrics typically demand that writing be merely compliant (even if it is as boring as hell), we earn the predictable consequences: dreary and safe writing—the opposite of fresh and fearless."[1]

When we are underwhelmed by student work and assessments, we have an opportunity to shift the purpose of the assessment from earning a grade to creating something inspiring, meaningful, and public.

Ron Berger, chief academic officer of EL Education, also speaks to the problems with turning in work to a teacher audience. In an article for Edutopia called "Deeper Learning: Highlighting Student Work," Berger notes:

> In all of my years sitting in classrooms as a student, in public schools that were highly regarded, I never once produced anything that resembled authentic work or had value beyond addressing a class requirement. My time was spent on an academic treadmill of turning in short assignments completed individually as final drafts—worksheets, papers, math problem sets, lab reports—none of which meant much to anyone and none of which resembled the work I have done in the real world. Although I received

1 Grant Wiggins, "EJ in Focus: Real-World Writing: Making Purpose and Audience Matter," *English Journal* 98, no. 5 (2009): 29–37.

good grades, I have no work saved from my days in school, because nothing I created was particularly original, important or beautiful.[2]

When we are underwhelmed by student work and assessments, it is an opportunity to shift the purpose of the assessment from earning a grade to creating something inspiring, meaningful, and public.

Imagine if students found our assessments original, important, and beautiful? How much more purpose would there be in our classrooms? To get to a place where students believe our work is authentic, we have to shift from compliance to engagement and from a teacher audience to a public audience.

John Spencer, the author of *Launch*, provides a helpful lens for thinking about the layers of authenticity.[3] This may be helpful if you teach very young students, as sometimes, privacy is a concern when sharing work publicly. In his Level 1, students reflect and create work in private. In Level 2, work is shared within the classroom but not beyond it. Level 2 is typical of most school assessments, as the work is semiprivate and shared with partners, small groups, and the teacher. In Level 3, students share their work with other classes or the whole school—extending their reach beyond the classroom walls. Spencer notes that although the work is not totally public in Level 3, the audience is still bigger than the immediate classroom, so this may be a goal for young students. In Level 4, students share their work publicly—with the world through blogs, podcasts, TED Talks, and in collaborations with real

2 Ron Berger, "Deeper Learning: Highlighting Student Work," George Lucas Educational Foundation, January 3, 2013, edutopia.org/blog/deeper-learning-student-work-ron-berger.

3 John Spencer, "What Happens When Students Launch Their Work to an Audience?," November 20, 2020, spencerauthor.com/launch-virtual/.

people who can critique and comment on the work. When students share their work publicly in Level 4, they experience multiple benefits including:

- They grow more empathetic.
- They work harder because the work has a deeper meaning.
- They develop a growth mindset. As they engage in the revision process, they develop resiliency.
- They learn to listen to criticism. In fact, they explicitly seek it out as a part of the revision process.
- They become fearless in their creative work.
- They engage in iterative thinking as they work through revisions to improve their work.
- They make connections between the learning and their world.
- They find their creative voice.[4]

If we want to increase student engagement and purpose, we need to create authentic opportunities for them to share their work with a real audience. At first, we may transition from Level 2 to Level 3 by creating gallery walks and schoolwide celebrations of student work, but when we can make work more public, there is an incredible opportunity to maximize purpose and pride.

Having an authentic audience is a key component of project-based learning (PBL), which we discuss in Workflow #10, but we don't need to design a full project-based unit to have an authentic audience. In this chapter, we will discuss strategies for ensuring that student work has opportunities to be published, as opposed to merely submitted to you for feedback or a grade.

4 Ibid.

Strategy #1: RAFT

Have students codesign a role-audience-format-topic (RAFT) assessment.[5] Within a RAFT, students make choices about who they are as creators, who their audience is, which format they want to use, and, finally, what task they want to complete, or the purpose of the assessment, aligned to the standard under study.

The *role* of the writer or creator in a RAFT is who students become when they are completing the assessment. Often, students are writing or creating as themselves, but in certain circumstances, they may assume another role for effect. For example, if students want to inform people of the impact of climate change, they may write a letter from the perspective of the Earth.

The *audience* is who they are writing to or creating for. Are they informally posting on social media? Writing formally to a person of importance? This is when students have to consider the audience and build empathy to consider what the audience needs.

The *format* is the genre, or form, of the response. Will students write a letter? Record a video public service announcement? Could they create a social media page? Create a piece of art for a local studio? Could they make a public speech on a TED-Ed stage? The answer will be largely dependent on their audience. What is the best way to reach the audience and accomplish the students' intended purpose?

Lastly, students need to consider the *task*. In a traditional RAFT, the T stands for "topic + strong verb," which really means "What's the point?" Why are they completing the assessment? Are they writing to persuade someone to take a certain course of action, or do they simply want to inform an audience about a new opportunity? Not only do they need to choose a purpose, but they need to take it a step further and consider why they personally are completing the

5 Carol Minnick Santa, Lynn T. Havens, and Bonnie J. Valdes, *Project CRISS: Creating Independence Through Student-Owned Strategies* (Dubuque, IA: Kendall Hunt, 2004).

assessment. This reason needs to be more important than receiving a grade.

You can make a copy, modify, and share the RAFT planning document pictured in Figure 18 to support students as they think through their role, audience, format, and task. In the early stages of preparing to write or create for an audience, students will benefit from additional support as they think through the parts of RAFT. We suggest dedicating time to conferencing with individuals or small groups of students about their responses to the questions on this document in the early stages of the assignment or project.

Imagine a middle school team is implementing an interdisciplinary unit on the environmental impact of human waste as well as ways to mitigate that impact through innovative technology. In a more traditional unit, students would complete a final project that would be shared with the teacher and maybe the rest of the class. The project would have one specific focus area—say, the importance of shifting to solar energy or composting. In a RAFT, students choose their role, an authentic audience, their format, and their task. You could have blank templates where you work with small groups of students in a station rotation model, or you can encourage individual students to add a role, audience, or project to a shared document as a component of a playlist. Using the following example, one student may write a proposal to move to single-stream recycling and send it to the Department of Recycling and Waste Management. Another student might craft a narrative from the perspective of the Earth, record a short animated film, and submit it to a student film festival.

Table 7 is a sample RAFT where students can mix and match to create hundreds of possible prompts. We recommend completing the chart with students instead of doing all the work ahead of time.

Figure 18: RAFT Planning Document

RAFT	
Role: The **role** is the person you become when you are completing this assessment. Will you write or create as yourself or will you become someone or something else for effect?	
Audience: The **audience** is who you are writing/creating for. Are you writing/creating informally (e.g., social media audience) or are you writing/creating for a formal audience (e.g., prestigious publication or famous person)? What will you need to know about your audience to write/create for them?	
Format: The **format** is the genre or form that the writing or creation will take to reach the intended audience. Will you write a letter, create a social media page, record a public service announcement, or design a piece of art for a local studio?	
Task: The **task** is the topic, which really means, "What's the point?" Why are you completing the assessment? How is this assessment meaningful to you? Are you writing to persuade someone to take a certain course of action, or did you create something to inform an audience about a new opportunity?	

Table 7: Sample RAFT

Role	Audience	Format *Must be published in a public space	Task
Self	Department of Recycling and Waste Management	Formal written letter	To prompt the audience to interact with you
The Earth	Voters in the town	TED-Ed Talk to submit to TED-Ed convention	To convince the audience to take action and change their habits or practices
Future citizens of the Earth	Grown-ups at home	Futuristic narrative of what happens if we don't have action (e.g., screenplay, stage play, book proposal)	To convince the audience to think differently

Strategy #2: Build Empathy for Your Real Audience

When students write for an audience of one (the teacher), they often focus on the outcomes of the rubric as opposed to considering the importance of the authentic audience. Wiggins provides the following questions to prompt empathy in determining the best way to write for an audience.

- Who is this audience?
- What are their expectations, needs, and interests? (Not your half-baked assumptions and projections, but the reality) [6]

These two questions not only help students build perspective-taking, a key component of social-emotional learning, but they also provide purpose that goes beyond a rubric. If you use a RAFT, you can create small groups based on the audience that students selected. Answering the questions will require students to research more about their audience or commit to interviewing members of the audience for perspective. We've adapted the questions from a toolkit for nonprofit organizations to provide a lens for students to learn more about their audience in Table 8.[7] Encourage students to answer the questions using multiple means of action and expression and to analyze how the outcomes of the questions will impact the development of their product.

6 Wiggins, "EJ in Focus: Real-World Writing."

7 Top Non-Profits, "Know Your Target Audience: 10 Questions to Ask," 2021, topnonprofits.com/know-your-target-audience-10-questions-to-ask/.

Table 8: Learn More about Your Audience

Learn More about Your Audience	
1. What is the desired action of your target audience?	
2. What are the demographics of your target audience? Create a bio of your target audience.	
3. What are the values, interests, hobbies, and lifestyles of your target audience?	
4. What needs, challenges, and frustrations do they have? How do you know?	
5. How does your idea, proposed action, or product help your target audience?	
6. How will you reach your target audience?	

Strategy #3: Gallery Walks, Expositions, and Engaging Your Audience

Just as students need support and onboarding to develop the skills necessary to write or create for an authentic audience, they also benefit from baby steps when sharing their work with other people and helping their audience engage with their work. Gallery walks or expositions offer a simple strategy for sharing work while also limiting the scope of who can view that work. Depending on who you choose to invite to a gallery walk or exposition, this approach to publishing student work could fall into Spencer's Level 2 (shared within the classroom) or Level 3 (shared with other classes or the larger school community). We have hosted gallery walks that kept work semiprivate and encouraged students to view and respond to each other's finished products. We have also invited other classes or even parents into a gallery walk or exhibition to view student work, making it more public.

During a gallery walk, the room is set up to allow each student or group to display their work. Ideally, there is a clear path around the room that students walk to view each other's work. Some teachers ask that gallery walks be silent so students can interact with multimedia elements on display and provide each other with thoughtful feedback. A gallery walk can also take a virtual format if students post their work in a shared digital space, like a portfolio page on the class LMS or a shared digital slide deck. Once students have their work displayed, much like art in a gallery, the work speaks for itself. To ensure the audience engages with the various pieces, you can ask students to place a printed QR code next to their work with a video introducing the piece or linking to a digital form with questions they would like their peers to answer. A feedback form can be digital or printed, depending on the individual student's preferences. You may want to give students a minimum number of pieces you want them to provide feedback on as they walk through the gallery of their peers' work.

An exposition is slightly different from a gallery walk because students typically stand beside their work to "present" it to the audience. They might give a talk, describe the parts of a process or model, present findings from an experiment they conducted or research they collected, provide a demonstration, or perform an original piece. An exposition challenges students to practice their speaking (as they present their work) and listening (as they view work) skills. The students get to interact with their audience in a more dynamic way during an exposition. Typically, teachers will split the exposition time in half so half of the class presents while the other half, along with any additional classes, parents, or community members, serves as the audience. Then the two groups switch roles, with the presenters becoming the audience members.

Since a gallery walk or an exposition is the final step in a summative assessment process, you might choose to use one of Project Zero's Thinking Routines as a strategy to get students thinking more deeply about the work on display as opposed to providing more traditional peer feedback.[8] Feedback is wonderful when students act on it to improve a piece, but it is less effective when focused on finished products that students will not continue to improve or revise. By contrast, Project Zero's Thinking Routines are designed to guide students in making their thinking visible.

Our favorite Thinking Routines to pair with a gallery walk or exposition are 1) See, Think, Wonder; 2) Connect, Extend, Challenge; and 3) I Used to Think, Now I Think. We've taken these three Thinking Routines and created a digital slide deck for each that you can copy, modify, and use with your students. These slides can be saved as PDFs and printed if you want to give students the option to capture their thinking digitally or handwrite their responses.

The See, Think, Wonder Thinking Routine, shown in Figure 19, can be used across grade levels and works particularly well for visual creations, like infographics, digital stories, artwork, graphic novels or comics, informational videos, or 3-D models. As students observe each other's work, they are encouraged to describe what they are seeing, surface their thinking about it, and articulate their wonderings or questions. This provides the creator of the work with invaluable insight into the clarity and effectiveness of their work as well as the impact that it had on their audience. What did their audience notice? What visually "popped" or stood out to them? What ideas or feelings did this work spark in the audience? What was the audience left wondering or curious about? Was anything unclear as the audience engaged with the work?

8 Project Zero, "PZ's Thinking Routines Toolbox," Harvard University Graduate School of Education, accessed March 5, 2022. pz.harvard.edu/thinking-routines.

Figure 19: Project Zero's See, Think, Wonder Thinking Routine in a Digital Slide Deck

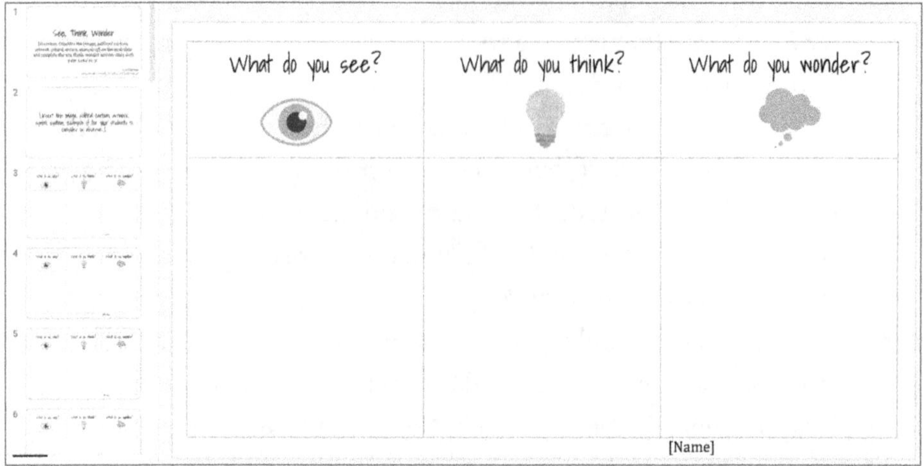

The Connect, Extend, Challenge Thinking Routine, shown in Figure 20, is ideal for work that presents new information, provides a different perspective, or challenges students' thinking on a topic. For example, students may present findings from a lab or experiment they designed to test an idea or a research-based argumentative essay they wrote on a social issue. As students engage with new ideas, they must connect what they are learning to what they already knew before this gallery walk or exposition. What prior knowledge did they have on this topic? Where did they learn what they know about this topic? Then they must consider how this information is extending or stretching their thinking. Finally, they must articulate what is confusing or unclear, what is challenging their thinking, and what they are curious about or wondering. This helps the creator understand the impact of their work on their audience's thinking and understanding of a particular topic, subject, or issue.

Figure 20: Project Zero's Connect, Extend, Challenge Thinking Routine in a Digital Slide Deck

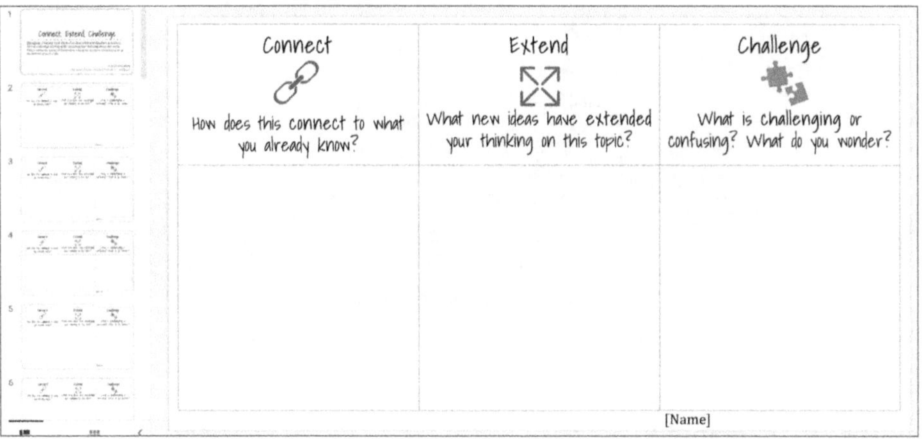

The I Used to Think, Now I Think Routine, shown in Figure 21, is excellent for building your students' metacognitive muscles. It challenges them to consider and articulate what they thought about a topic or issue *before* the gallery walk or exposition and describe how their thinking changed as a result of engaging with a particular piece of work. Did this piece of work cause their thinking to shift? If so, what about this piece impacted their thinking? Did it affirm their thoughts or opinions on a topic or issue? If so, why? This Thinking Routine helps the creator to understand the impact that their work had on the audience's thinking about their topic or issue. This can help creators to appreciate the power of the learning artifacts they are creating in your class and their potential effect on other people.

Figure 21: Project Zero's I Used to Think, Now I Think Thinking Routine in a Digital Slide Deck

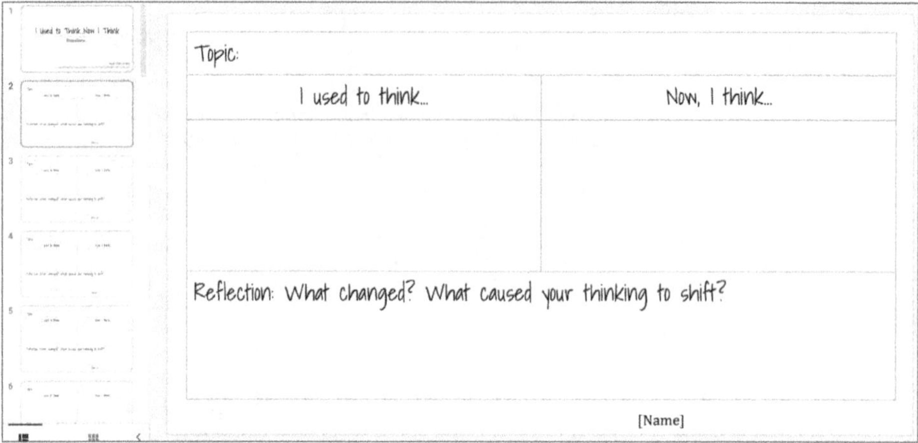

Regardless of the strategy your students use, they must learn how to engage their audience when they publish or share their work. It is audience engagement that helps students to appreciate the power of their voices and their creations. Feedback from an audience is motivating, shifting students from wanting their work to be "good enough" (which is common when the teacher is the only person viewing that work) to wanting their work to be *really* good.

You may want to spend the first few months of the school year on-boarding students to a variety of feedback strategies and Thinking Routines so they become familiar with each. Then you can gradually release responsibility to your students to select the strategy or collection of strategies they want to use to engage a particular audience. The goal should be to shift the decision-making around audience engagement to your students as they become more comfortable identifying the purpose of their work and understanding the intended audience for that work.

WRAP-UP

When students write or create for an audience of one, they may only care about the grade. When we shift to authentic audiences, students begin to think about how their work and the artifacts they create will impact others. This also helps to distribute the workload of providing feedback, as students can get feedback from authentic audiences and then make revisions to their work inspired by that feedback. Knowing that real people will be critiquing their work leads to increased purpose, ownership, empathy, and quality. Oh—and the bonus is less grading for us!

REFLECT AND DISCUSS

1. How many of your current assessments are designed for an audience of one? What is one assignment that you can shift to having a more authentic audience? How can you use the strategies in this chapter to make this transition?
2. How could you use or adapt the RAFT format to allow students to choose an authentic audience to share their work with?
3. Why is building empathy for an audience essential? What activities or routines could you implement to provide students with practice empathizing with a particular audience? Before a large-scale assignment or project, how might you use the "Learn More about Your Audience" resource to provide students practice with this skill?
4. Have you used gallery walks or expositions in the past? If so, which strategy did you use? Describe the experience. Did you invite people outside of your class to join the experience? If not, what might be the impact of inviting other classes, family, or community members?
5. What are your thoughts on using Project Zero's Thinking Routines as a strategy to engage an audience during a gallery

walk or exposition? How might these Thinking Routines benefit both the creator and the audience member?

PUT IT INTO ACTION

It's time to shift an assessment from an audience of one to an authentic audience. Transform one of your assignments or projects into an opportunity to connect your students to an actual audience. Use one of the strategies in this chapter to take your first steps!

- Strategy #1: RAFT
- Strategy #2: Build empathy for your real audience
- Strategy #3: Gallery walks, expositions, and engaging your audience

Planning Template 4: Authentic Audience

Assignment or Project Description: • What are the learning objectives? • What are the expectations for this assignment or project?	
What strategy will you use? • RAFT • Building empathy • Gallery walk • Exposition • Engaging an audience with Thinking Routines	
What blended learning model or strategy will you use to shift control to students as they work on this assignment or project? • Station rotation model • Playlist model • Choice boards	
Feedback: • How can you create time and space to support students as they work on their assignments or projects? • How will you encourage the audience to provide feedback? Can students decide what type of feedback would be most useful?	
Student agency: • Will students get to make decisions about the content, process, or product? • Will students have a voice in determining the best audience for their work?	

WORKFLOW SHIFT #5

From Teacher-Created to Student-Generated Review and Practice

NFL Game Film

Catlin

My sister and I are big football fans. Despite growing up in Los Angeles, she is a die-hard Green Bay Packers fan, and I love the Seattle Seahawks and the San Francisco 49ers. We participate in two different fantasy football leagues, where we mix and match players from a variety of teams. So on Sundays you'll find us both watching RedZone and tracking the action happening across multiple games.

I need to pause here for a moment and just point out that the person who first conceived RedZone is a genius. It's all the action with none of the commercials. It's fast paced and exciting, cutting back and forth between games each time a team is in scoring position. The host, Scott Hanson, provides commentary on what is happening on the field, both on what players and teams are doing well and what isn't working.

Hanson's third-party perspective provides insight into the game that has helped to deepen my understanding, but most players learn by watching game film over and over and over. Players in the NFL have tablets loaded with footage designed to help them prepare for the game ahead. Malcolm Jenkins, a safety for the New Orleans Saints, says he watches two to three hours of game film every day on his own in addition to game films he watches in team meetings. Football players, particularly the defensive line, need to understand what to expect on game day as they face their rivals. They need to understand their opponent's tendencies, groupings, formations, and routes. What is the quarterback likely to do? Will he rely heavily on a running game or look to throw the ball? What routes does this team typically run? Where are the weaknesses in the offensive line, and how can defensive players exploit those weaknesses in a game?

Many of the best players in the NFL dedicate significant time beyond team meetings and practices to watching game film on their own to prepare for the game ahead. Each player has individual preferences when it comes to watching game film. Some watch for hours every day, and others limit their watching to forty-five minutes at a time, so they can digest what they've seen. Some watch while soaking in a tub after practice, and others project game film on a big screen at home. And different players study different parts of the game that are relevant to their specific positions. They know their assignments on game day and study the specific plays they will be part of and the players they will be facing off against. They do not need to watch every part of the game to prepare. In fact, watching every part of the game would waste their valuable time and dilute the effectiveness of studying game film. Instead, focusing on precise moments in the game that involve their position and the specific players they will face helps them mentally prepare by imagining likely scenarios and reviewing plays in their heads.

Like NFL players watch game film and study plays and players to prepare for a game, students need to engage in regular retrieval practice and review to deepen their content knowledge and hone their skills. This practice is most effective when it is woven into the fabric of the students' school day, not treated as an isolated event, and is personalized, targeting specific areas each student needs to focus on developing.

However, it is common to see practice relegated to a handful of days before an exam, when the focus is on cramming information into students' brains instead of focusing on pulling, or retrieving, information out, which brain-based research indicates is far more effective.

Like NFL players watch game film and study plays and players to prepare for a game, students need to engage in regular retrieval practice and review to deepen their content knowledge and hone their skills.

The Research and Reality: Tools to Power Up!

Reviewing and practicing concepts, processes, and skills should be an ongoing part of a student's experience in school. In *Powerful Teaching: Unleash the Science of Learning*, Pooja K. Agarwal and Patrice Bain apply brain-based research to education to help teachers improve instructional practices and boost student learning. They describe four evidence-based strategies that they call "power tools." These include retrieval practice, spacing, interleaving, and feedback-driven metacognition.[1]

Retrieval practice is the process of deliberately recalling information that we already know. Think about it in the context of cooking. Each time we reach into our spice racks to grab the paprika

1 Pooja K. Agarwal and Patrice Bain, *Powerful Teaching: Unleash the Science of Learning* (Indianapolis, IN: John Wiley & Sons: 2019).

or the garlic salt, we are able to locate it faster than the last time we needed it. Similarly, the more we revisit a specific book on our bookshelf, the easier it is to find it the next time. The same thing happens for students when they engage in retrieval practice. As they intentionally and repeatedly pull information out of their memory, they get better at retrieving it in the future.

Spacing encourages educators to make practice a process that is a regular part of their lessons, instead of an event. Just as football players watch game film every week, analyzing plays and players in preparation for a big game, students need repeated practice with retrieval over time. The more frequently and consistently they revisit concepts and skills, the more likely they are to retain that information and successfully apply those skills in the future.

Interleaving is a technique where different concepts, topics, or types of practice are mixed together. The goal is to avoid rote learning that is not adaptable. Football players don't just practice one play at a time, they mix it up to better prepare for games where anything can happen. If they only prepared for one scenario, they would not be nearly as effective in responding to different plays. Similarly, students need to practice with a variety of topics and types of questions in order to "tease out patterns and form connections."[2] When using interleaving as a technique to mix up review and practice, "the learning tasks become more intellectually taxing and time-consuming, requiring kids to slow down and mentally toggle through lots of information, making connections in their thinking before arriving at the appropriate strategies to solve a problem." So, less is more when it comes to interleaving.

The fourth and final power tool described in *Powerful Teaching* is **feedback-driven metacognition**. The goal of feedback-driven metacognition is for students to discern what they know from what

2 Hoa P. Nguyen, "How to Use Interleaving to Foster Deeper Learning," George Lucas Educational Foundation, June 11, 2021, edutopia.org/article/how-use-interleaving-foster-deeper-learning.

they do not know, developing a heightened awareness of their content knowledge, skills, and abilities. Feedback on retrieval practice tells a student what answers or responses were correct and which were incorrect, so they have a clearer picture of their strengths and the areas that need more time and attention. This feedback, whether generated by a machine, given by a teacher, or gained through self-assessment, increases the student's understanding of their progress as a learner.

These four brain-based power tools can guide more effective approaches to review and practice, especially when we think about positioning the student at the center of the learning experience. The more ownership students take over their review and practice, the more likely it is to be personalized to their specific needs and become a sustainable part of their work in a classroom.

Traditional approaches to engaging students in retrieval practice are problematic on several fronts.

1. Review and practice are often focused on preparing for an exam instead of treated as an integral part of every class.
2. Review and practice often encourage rote memorization instead of requiring that students develop adaptability and flexibility.
3. The teacher does the lion's share of the work by creating review questions and practice activities for retrieval practice or compiling a long list of items to include on study guides.
4. A single review game or study guide does not provide "spacing" or repeated exposure to vocabulary, concepts, or skills.
5. The person generating a review game, practice problems, or a study guide is the one doing the critical thinking.

Strategy #1: Student-Created Review Questions

Online review games are a popular way of providing students with review and practice that is gamified, offering students immediate feedback on their accuracy and providing teachers with quick data on student performance. Kahoot! and similar review software can be used to integrate review into an online station, as a class game during a whole-group rotation, or as a formative assessment mechanism built into a playlist.

Generating a variety of high-quality questions for a review game is a time-consuming affair and requires higher-level thinking. Too often this task falls on the teacher. We think this is a missed opportunity. Instead of spending hours creating a collection of review games, you can group students to work collaboratively to generate a collection of questions. Groups can decide what they want to focus on and the types of questions they want to design. You can allow them to make key decisions about the content or skills they focus on, since retrieval practice should encourage students to return to concepts, processes, vocabulary, and skills from different points in the curriculum.

When students develop the questions, they must think critically about the content they've covered and target essential vocabulary, concepts, and skills. This collaborative activity is ideal for a small group as part of a station rotation or whole-group rotation lesson. Ask groups to work together to craft a collection of questions on paper or a digital slide deck, like the one in Figure 22. They can use the features inside of the deck to create a variety of different types of questions that include media and combine different formats: short answer, matching, multiple choice, ranking, and true/false.

Figure 22: Student-Designed Review Questions Slide Deck

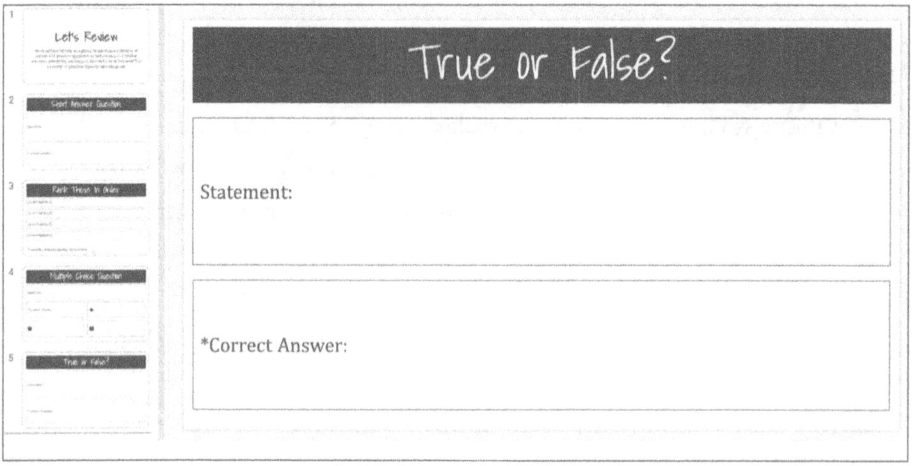

True or False?

Statement:

*Correct Answer:

After students have designed a collection of questions, you can pick and choose the strongest ones to create a review game for the entire class. If you want students to have more control over the questions they work on to ensure that the retrieval practice meets their specific needs, you can share one group's collection of questions with another group and ask them to select a certain number of questions to answer. That way, they can focus on questions that will be most helpful to them in reviewing key concepts, vocabulary, and skills. Remember that mixing concepts during retrieval practice is more mentally taxing, so students will not need a large quantity of questions for this to be an effective exercise. In fact, it may be more effective to pair the students' selection of questions with a reflective prompt asking them to explain why they chose to focus on particular questions.

Once they've reflected on their choices and completed the practice, you (or the group that developed the questions) should provide an answer key so students can assess the accuracy of their work to determine what they did well, which questions they answered correctly, and which questions they missed and need to spend time reviewing. They can also reflect on what they learned from this exercise. What concepts, processes, formulas, etc. do they remember and understand? Where do they need to spend more time practicing? Where are they noticing growth or improvement? What additional support might help them to continue to improve? These reflections can take a variety of forms, so give your students agency to decide how they want to share their reflections.

Strategy #2: Student-Created Review and Practice Choice Board

Choice boards prioritize student agency, allowing learners to decide which activities to spend time on; however, they can be time-consuming to create. If the purpose of a choice board is to give students the opportunity to select concepts, vocabulary, and skills to review and practice prior to an assessment, we encourage teachers to ask students to work collaboratively to design a review and practice choice board, like the template in Figure 23. These student-designed boards are a great alternative to the traditional teacher-created study guide.

Creating a dynamic review and practice choice board for their peers is a cognitively challenging task for students. They have to think about the learning cycle or unit and identify key vocabulary, concepts, and skills needed to be successful on an assessment. Then they have to design various activities that are likely to appeal to different types of learners to ensure their peers have meaningful choices. This is a rigorous task, so it's a good idea to strategically pair or group students for peer support to ensure they produce a meaningful product.

If you are using the station rotation model, we suggest dedicating two or three stations to this task, depending on the length of the station work and your students' progress. Students may want to create their boards on paper or in a digital document. You can collect the finished boards, review the content, and select the strongest boards to use for review and practice. Then you can have the whole class work to complete items on the choice boards during a whole-group rotation or as part of a playlist. As students work to complete learning activities from the board, you can pull individual or small groups of students for personalized instruction or support ahead of an assessment.

Figure 23: Review and Practice Student-Created Choice Board

Review & Practice Choice Board		
Choose an item from each column to prepare for the assessment.		
Vocabulary	Key Concepts	Skills

Strategy #3: Prepare for Standardized Assessments

Preparing students for classroom assessments is critical, but we also are aware of the reality of the state standardized tests, SATs, IB exams, AP tests, and other high-stakes tests. In these instances, students aren't focused on a unit of study but rather a culmination of everything they have already learned over the course of multiple years. Still, UDL and blended learning can help students to feel more confident in sharing what they know. The recipe for test preparation involves the following ingredients:

- As many practice tests as you can get your hands on
- Exemplars of previous student work, if the powers that be in the testing industry provide them
- Rubrics available for open-ended responses
- Research on how multiple-choice questions are designed
- Research on test anxiety and how to avoid it

Of course, you could find all these ingredients yourself, but you're far enough into this book to know that we recommend shifting that task to students. One idea is to create small groups and assign each group a task. Table 9 can be used or adapted to give students their marching orders.

After each group has completed their research, they can prepare a presentation, a class activity, or a review game to help make the process of taking the standardized test more transparent. You also have a document that students have access to throughout the year. You can encourage them to connect back to it as they draft their own review questions, revisit exemplars of student work, compare and contrast their writing to examples, and study the tips and tricks of multiple-choice question design.

Table 9: Group-Generated Prep for Standardized Tests

Solving the Standardized-Testing Puzzle	
In May, you will be taking the [fill in the name of the test]. You will be prepared with all the knowledge and skills you need to answer the questions. To help you feel super confident, it is also important that you know the rules of the test you're going to take. Succeeding on standardized tests is like solving a puzzle. In this class, groups will collaborate to figure out a piece of the puzzle, and then we will create an action plan that brings all the pieces together!	
	Directions
Group 1	Find **practice tests** for our grade/subject area. Link to them in the column on the left. Once you have identified as many tests as you can find, review them all and notice what they have in common. Create a concept map, short presentation, or written piece that highlights features of the tests that you can share with your classmates.
Group 2	Identify **exemplars of high-quality written student work** for the test you will take. Once you identify at least five examples, review them all and notice what they have in common. Create a concept map, short presentation, or recipe of the features and patterns of exemplary writing.
Group 3	**Locate the rubrics** that are used to grade open-ended responses. Once you find the rubrics, create a resource where you link student work to each of the performance categories so there are both examples and nonexamples. You can get high-quality examples from Group 2, but you will need to find examples of all other performance categories on your own. After you find an example for each category, write a reflection about what the piece was missing.

Group 4	Writing high-quality **multiple-choice questions** is an art and a science. What are some of the ways that test designers write questions that confuse or trick the test takers? Create a tool, presentation, video/audio, or written piece where you share how test creators make tricky multiple-choice questions and share strategies for the best ways to ace a multiple-choice test! As a group, research more about how to write high-quality multiple-choice questions.
Group 5	Some people get **test anxiety** when they sit for a standardized exam. As a group, research more about test anxiety and how to take steps to minimize it. Create a tool, presentation, video/audio, or written piece where you share what test anxiety is and how to work to avoid it.

WRAP-UP

If we want students to be more expert and reflective in their learning, we need to shift responsibility for review and practice to them. As educators, we spend so much time creating study guides, writing review questions, and making review games when our students are capable of doing the work themselves. Just think—instead of staying up all night making that *Jeopardy!* game, you could be watching the actual show! When we help students take ownership of their own review and practice, we also make the assessment process more transparent and help them build confidence. Just as NFL players continually review videos, our students need to continually review their learning, make predictions about how they will be assessed, and navigate the world of standardized testing.

REFLECT AND DISCUSS

1. How do your current practices compare to the evidence on the importance of retrieval practice, spacing, interleaving, and feedback-driven metacognition?

2. How do student-generated choice boards allow students to personalize their review and practice in universally designed classrooms?
3. Consider your current practices for preparing students for more standardized assessments. How would those practices look different if you were to implement the strategies outlined in this chapter?

PUTTING IT INTO PRACTICE

It's time to give your review and practice strategies a UDL and BL makeover. Instead of scheduling a test review day where you create a study guide and review games yourself, consider trying one of the following strategies.

- Strategy #1: Student-created review questions
- Strategy #2: Student-created review and practice choice board
- Strategy #3: Prepare for standardized assessments

Be sure to reflect with students on the effectiveness of the transition and how it impacts their engagement and level of preparedness when it's time for them to share what they know on a summative assessment.

Planning Template 5: Student-Generated Review + Practice

What content are students creating the review and practice for? • Unit • Learning cycle • AP exam • Standardized exam	
What strategy will you use? • Student-created review questions • Student-created review and practice choice board • Prepare for standardized assessments	
What blended learning model or strategy will you use to shift control to students? • Station rotation model • Choice boards • Playlist model • Whole-group rotation model	
How will you use your time while students work to create review and practice activities for each other? • Provide personalized instruction and support • Give focused, actionable feedback on their review and practice activities • Conduct conferences about student progress	
How will you encourage students to reflect on the impact of this activity on their engagement and level of preparedness to take the assessment?	

WORKFLOW SHIFT #6

From Formative Assessment as Teacher Tool to a Metacognitive Tool for Learners

Succumbing to the Apple Watch

Katie

I held off on getting an Apple Watch for as long as I could. As my friends added small computers to their wrists, I objected. My closest friends were infatuated with the fitness app, symbolized by three colorful concentric circles that represent the time you spend standing, the amount of activity you get in a day, and the amount of exercise. The idea is to "close your rings" every day by meeting goals in each category. To be honest, I thought the idea was ridiculous. Things escalated one night as we huddled in Kate's home office, dubbed The Ladies Lounge, enjoying a glass of wine and playing hearts on her glass coffee table. Long after hearts were broken, Kate received a notification from the Fitness app that it was time to stand up. And you know where this is going. She stood. Yep, it was official. I would never get an Apple Watch.

As I share this story, an Apple Watch is on my left wrist. In all fairness, I didn't buy it for myself. One day, I went to my room upstairs and found a wrapped box on my bedside table. Now I'm hooked.

When I first learned about the Apple Watch, I was thinking of the Fitness App in terms of the information Apple was getting. I saw it as a marketing tool, collecting data *about* me but not *for* me. I could not see how any information on that watch would impact me in any way or change my habits. I was wrong.

As soon as I received the watch, I turned off most of the notifications. I didn't want to receive phone calls, access emails, or get constant reminders about texts. I have plenty of those when I'm on my phone or logged into my computer. I used the watch as—wait for it—a watch. And that suited me just fine. A couple of days after I joined team smart watch, I had a tête-à-tête with my ten-year-old daughter. I could feel myself getting frustrated when, suddenly, my wrist pulsed. I looked down at my watch and saw a reminder to breathe. The watch sensed my pulse increasing (and goodness knows what else), and it sent me a little reset. I laughed, took a deep breath, and was able to cope much better with the conversation about whether hair brushing should be optional.

I also started appreciating the reminders to stand up. There are some days when I spend hours sitting—writing, presenting, coaching, or providing feedback on assessments in my graduate courses. I fall into a state of flow and completely forget to get up and stretch, have a glass of water, and take the dog out. I'm not competitive about closing my circles, and I still don't have any notifications from email or my phone, but the information is a tool for me to be more aware of my breathing, my sitting habits, and how much activity I am getting.

I have been a runner for over thirty years and generally didn't think much about collecting feedback during my runs. Before my watch, I would download an audiobook, plug in my earbuds, stash my phone in my running belt, and try to push myself running, having no real measure of success other than the distance I ran. Once I got my watch, I started to be more purposeful and motivated in my running life. I noticed my average pace and started to push it when I was feeling confident. I can tell when I'm pushing it too hard from my heart rate monitor. When my watch tells me to breathe, I can slow down and take a stretch. The best part? No more clunky running belt—my audiobooks are on my wrist!

I have come around to using the Apple Watch as a tool. As I reflect on how quickly that happened, I also think about the potential for formative assessments to be transformed. Too often, formative assessments seem like we are collecting data *about* students but not *for* them. Quizzes, class participation, and homework are often seen as grades that are necessary for learning, but the intent is often *not* learning. Rather, it's often an accountability or compliance tool. We sometimes hear that "if we don't grade it, they won't take it seriously." When we use formative assessment as a "carrot," its purpose doesn't extend too far beyond a number plugged into a grade book.

As we unpack the purpose of formative assessments, remember the story of my watch. We need to design assessments as tools that students can customize and use to reflect on their own learning so *they* can take action. Maybe they won't be taking deep breaths or taking a walk around the block, but they will build self-awareness, self-reflection, and executive function to use what they are learning about themselves as learners to "close the rings" on their version of success.

The Research and Reality: Assessment as Learning

Think back to your school years. How many of you remember your teacher announcing that there would be a pop quiz? Maybe some of you felt prepared and actually enjoyed this type of announcement, but we can guess a pop quiz would send many of you into full panic mode. When we were in school, pop quizzes, homework assignments, and other formative assessments were something to be dreaded and feared. And, regardless of success or failure, does anyone ever remember what they learned from those pop quizzes? What was their purpose, exactly?

In *UDL and Blended Learning*, we discussed formative assessments *as* learning, as opposed to assessments *of* learning. Too often, assessments are used as measurement tools as opposed to reflection tools. Since we are all in the business of learning, it is critical that our formative assessments drive instruction and foster expert learning.

Too often, assessments are used as measurement tools as opposed to reflection tools. Since we are all in the business of learning, it is critical that our formative assessments drive instruction and foster expert learning.

Much of the work on formative assessments has been informed by the research of Paul Black and Dylan Wiliam in their seminal article "Inside the Black Box: Raising Standards through Classroom Assessment." They identify the main features of formative assessment as sharing criteria with learners, developing classroom talk and questioning, giving appropriate feedback, and peer and self-assessment.[1]

Sharing Criteria with Learners

When we share criteria with learners, we connect to UDL's emphasis on firm goals. We have to be clear about what all learners need to know and do to work with students to define success criteria. Traditionally, teachers take the lead on creating success criteria, but when we commit to expert learning, we can empower students to create their own definitions of success.

When students create their own success criteria, it enables them to better understand what teachers expect them to know and do,

1 Paul Black and Dylan Wiliam, "Inside the Black Box: Raising Standards through Classroom Assessment," *Phi Delta Kappan* 80, no. 2: 144, 146–48.

which "allows students to support each other and take responsibility for their own learning by helping them accurately and appropriately evaluate learning against shared expectations and make any necessary adjustments to the learning. Students become activated as learners."[2]

Developing Classroom Talk and Questioning

When formative assessments are used as measurement tools to judge performance, they don't create an environment where students are apt to discuss misconceptions and make plans for improvement. Rather, students lay their bodies atop quiz grades, shielding them from wandering eyes and nosy neighbors.

If we want to encourage students to share the results of formative assessments, we have to stress that the purpose of the assessments and the discussion that follows is reflection and collective planning. One of our favorite videos is of middle-school math teacher Leah Alcala from the Teaching Channel. In the video "Highlighting Mistakes: A Grading Strategy," she models her strategy for using quizzes as formative assessments. She no longer puts grades on assessments, but rather provides feedback by highlighting mistakes without sharing the reason for the highlighting.[3] Imagine how much faster you could get through correcting if you only highlighted mistakes?

She notes, "I want every interaction I have with a kid to be a learning moment. What I was finding when I was handing back tests the old way, when I put a grade on it, [was that] kids would look at their grade, decide if they were good at math or not, and then would never look at it again." I think all of us have those moments: we spend

2 Kathy Dyer, "What You Need to Know When Establishing Success Criteria in the Classroom," Teach. Learn. Grow. NWEA, August 4, 2020, nwea.org/blog/2018/what-you-need-to-know-when-establishing-success-criteria-in-the-classroom/.

3 Leah Alcala, "Highlighting Mistakes: A Grading Strategy," video, 7:00, The Teaching Channel, 2015, learn.teachingchannel.com/video/math-test-grading-tips.

so much time providing feedback, and our hard work is immediately stuffed into recycling bins and binders, never to be seen again.

Alcala recognized that the grades on the formative assessments become a barrier to learning, so she transitioned to highlighting mistakes and misconceptions and encouraged groups of students to work together to determine what the mistake was and how they could work together to fix it. Although she does this by having groups work simultaneously, the station rotation model could be used so teachers can observe each small group and address any misconceptions.

In the video, as they work in their groups, students share the results of the formative assessment and ask questions like "What did you do here?" as they compare answers, reflect on instructional materials, and teach each other. Alcala notes that when she hands back the assessments "students are continuing to learn"—which is the purpose of assessments, after all. After students have grappled with their quizzes, they can retake the assessment. If you haven't seen the video, it is a tremendous example of the potential of formative assessments to drive instruction, collaboration, and continued learning.

Appropriate Feedback, Peer and Self-Assessment

In Leah Alcala's class, students provide each other with feedback as they discuss their misconceptions and highlighted mistakes. It is important to note how the feedback is formative-oriented as opposed to summative-oriented. When feedback is summative-oriented, there is less likelihood that it will change the quality of learners' performance, as there is less room for them to redo or rethink their work.[4] Because Alcala facilitated small-group discussion in the process of formative assessment, the feedback that students received

4 Khalid Said and Abdelouahid El Mouzrati, "Investigating Teacher Written Corrective Feedback as a Formative Assessment Tool," *Arab World English Journal* 9 no. 4: 232–41.

from the teacher, each other, and their own reflection was productive and yielded improved outcomes.

Even with these features, many formative assessments are thought of as events, like giving a quiz or having a discussion, instead of as a "more integral and symbiotic process."[5] When formative assessments are seen as a process of student reflection, self-assessment, feedback, and action planning, students build more ownership of their learning process.

When formative assessments are seen as a process of student reflection, self-assessment, feedback, and action planning, students build more ownership of their learning process.

When formative assessments include transparent criteria, encourage classroom talk, and provide feedback to learners about their process, students can translate the results into action to build understanding and skills that are under construction.[6] When they don't include these components, they are mini summative assessments moonlighting as formative assessments—a practice we need to transform.

In this chapter, you will learn that our focus doesn't have to be on changing the content of formative assessments as much as shifting the process of formative assessments. You might still provide traditional quizzes or check-ins, but they can be used as catalysts for self-reflection, discussion, and feedback—not a tool for grading or compliance. The strategies we outline in this chapter align with core features of formative assessment as shared in the research, with a UDL and blended learning twist.

5 Shuichi Ninomiya, "The Possibilities and Limitations of Assessment for Learning: Exploring the Theory of Formative Assessment and the Notion of 'Closing the Learning Gap,'" *Educational Studies in Japan: International Yearbook* 79, no. 10: 79–91.

6 Hem Chand Dayal, "How Teachers Use Formative Assessment Strategies during Teaching: Evidence from the Classroom," *Australian Journal of Teacher Education* 46, no. 7: 1–21.

Strategy #1: Co-create Criteria with Learners Using Multiple Means

As teachers, we often tell our students what success looks like instead of empowering them to explore exemplars and determine what it looks like for themselves. When we share an example that models our expectations for an assessment or a project, we often take for granted that students recognize what makes the work exceptional. This is not to say that we cannot provide exemplars. Rather, when we share them, we should ask students to work collaboratively to articulate *why* they are examples of success. This is critical for expert learning. As an adult, if you wanted to submit a manuscript to an education publication, it would be valuable to first read examples of some of the publisher's previous work. One excellent example of determining success criteria is the book *How to Deliver a TED Talk: Secrets of the World's Most Inspiring Presentations* by Jeremy Donovan. He notes,

> Commenting on an earlier version of this book, a reviewer wrote something along the lines of "You don't need to buy this book if you just watch the top 10 TED Talks and then watch the ones that aren't as popular to see the difference." That critic was correct! That said, my goal is to reveal the secrets and save you 20 years of studying public speaking and countless hours of watching and deconstructing hundreds of great and mediocre TED Talks.[7]

Although this response is a little saucy (which we love), we want to point out that he is willingly doing ALL the work for the reader when they are capable of doing it themselves. In this scenario, it makes sense. In your classroom, it does not. We need to transition from "writing the book," and instead shift the cognitive load to

7 Jeremy Donovan, *How to Deliver a TED Talk: Secrets of the World's Most Inspiring Presentations* (New York: McGraw Hill, 2014).

students using the principles of UDL. We can do this using multiple means. Students can analyze examples and nonexamples of texts, podcasts, videos, artistic representations, and class presentations. They can make connections using Venn diagrams, concept maps, writing, or sketching. Once they have worked to determine success criteria, they can compare and contrast their criteria with others' and create "recipes" for success. In short, they are writing their own book—which is more work for them, yes. But it is less work for you, and the process helps learners gain a better understanding of the goal and success criteria, their own performance, and what they may need to do to close the gap.

The process of exploring examples and nonexamples and then crafting clear success criteria will take time. It's best not to rush students through this process if we want it to be meaningful and yield high-quality outcomes. You may want to use the playlist model to design a sequence of learning activities, like the one in Figure 24, as a tool to allow students—individually, in pairs, or as part of a small group—to self-pace through this process.

The playlist model is ideal for any process or series of steps that will benefit from variable time on tasks. Exploring the examples and nonexamples to understand and identify the key characteristics of each will take learners different amounts of time, so they'll benefit from having more control over the pace at which they work.

It's also important to remember that designing a playlist requires a combination of online and offline learning. Even though most playlists are created online using a digital format, we want to include activities to give students a much-needed break from the screen and an opportunity to engage with their peers.

In addition to balancing the online with some offline activities, a playlist is more likely to keep students engaged if we also strive to balance individual tasks with opportunities for students to collaborate around shared tasks, like the process of articulating success criteria with a partner. These collaborative tasks give students the chance to share their learning and learn from one another.

A playlist can be integrated into a series of station rotation or whole-group-rotation lessons, or it can stand alone.

Figure 24: Playlist: Create Your Own Success Criteria

<table>
<tr><th colspan="2">Playlist: Create Your own Success Criteria</th></tr>
<tr><th>Directions</th><th>Your Work</th></tr>
<tr><td>Reflection:
• Why is it valuable for you to create your own success criteria?
• How might defining your own success criteria impact the quality of your work?</td><td>[Insert your text or a link]</td></tr>
<tr><td>Explore Examples & Nonexamples:
• Explore examples and nonexamples in a format that appeals to you.
<table><tr><th>Examples</th><th>Nonexamples</th></tr><tr><td>[insert links]</td><td>[insert links]</td></tr></table>As you explore, capture what you are noticing.
• Venn diagram
• Concept maps
• Writing
• Sketching</td><td>[Insert your text, image, or a link]</td></tr>
</table>

<table>
<tr>
<td>

Discuss:

- With a partner, as part of a small group, or online in a discussion forum, share what you learned with your peers.
    - What do the examples have in common? What features struck you as particularly strong in the examples you explored?
    - What did you notice about the nonexamples?
- How were they different from the examples?
- After engaging in a discussion, reflect on what you learned.

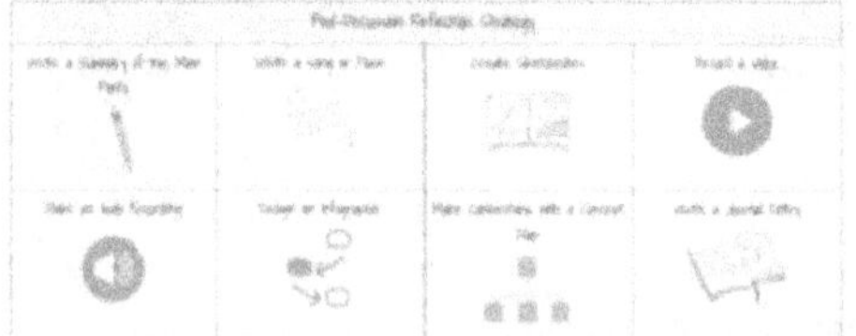

</td>
<td>

Success Criteria for ____________				
Criteria	1 Beginning	2 Developing	3 Proficient	4 Mastery

[Insert your text, image, or a link]

</td>
</tr>
<tr>
<td>

Create:

- With a partner or as part of a small group, identify three success criteria you want to focus on as you design your rubric.
- Work collaboratively to discuss then describe what the success criteria will look like at each level of mastery.

</td>
<td></td>
</tr>
<tr>
<td>

Reflection:

- What did you learn from this exercise? How do you think this process will impact how you approach this task?

</td>
<td></td>
</tr>
</table>

Strategy #2: Facilitate Classroom Discussion about Formative Assessments

Once students understand what success looks like, they can complete a formative assessment, like a draft of a written response or video, a multimedia presentation, or a more traditional assessment like a quiz. Once all students have completed this, they can be assessed by the teacher or a peer, or they can assess their own work in relation to the predetermined success criteria. This is when the discussion begins. We recommend you adapt the concept of an exam wrapper to drive discussion.

An exam wrapper is a common technique used in higher education where students are given prompts to reflect on before taking an assessment and again after they receive feedback on the assessment as a means to get them thinking about their study skills and learning. The questions "wrap" around the assessment to build more metacognitive reflection about learning. Such an exercise prompts students to think critically and constructively about their performance, guiding them to be more metacognitive, understanding their strengths, identifying areas in need of further development, and planning a more successful approach in the future.[8] Although exam wrappers are generally used on major exams, we advocate for using exam wrappers on formative assessments so students have time to reflect on their learning and their preparation strategies before it's time to apply learning on a summative assessment. A traditional exam wrapper may ask questions like the ones in Figure 25. Note that we are using these questions on a formative assessment.

8 Tara S. Carpenter, Lisa Carter Beall, and Linda C. Hodges, "Using a Learning Management System for Exam Wrapper Feedback to Prompt Metacognitive Awareness in Large Courses," *Journal of Teaching and Learning with Technology* 9 (special issue): 79–91.

Figure 25: Exam-Wrapper Questions

Exam Wrapper Discussion + Reflection Prompts	
Before the formative assessment 	After the formative assessment 
• How prepared do you feel to take this formative assessment? • What are the learning experiences we have had in this class that relate to the focus of this assessment? • Before you share what you know, what areas are you feeling confident in? • Before you share what you know, what specific concepts or skills are you feeling unsure of? • What did you do to prepare for this assessment? How helpful were these strategies?	• If you struggled to share what you have learned, what was the main reason why? • How will the results of this formative assessment impact how you prepare for the summative assessment? • What questions do you still have after reviewing the results of this formative assessment? • Did anything surprise you as you reviewed your results? • Did you notice growth or improvement in any areas? • What are your next steps in terms of acting on the results of this formative assessment?

The "before the assessment" questions can be used to facilitate small-group discussions or individual reflections as students prepare for a formative assessment. After they receive their results, they can compare them to the success criteria they created and then discuss or reflect on the "after the assessment" questions.

You can use the exam-wrapper approach to design a whole-group rotation that moves the class as a unit through a series of online and offline learning activities, as pictured in Figure 26. The class may begin with a welcome task (e.g., set a goal for the week) or bell ringer (e.g., retrieval practice). This could be online or offline, done individually or with a partner.

Once the welcome activity or bell ringer is complete and you've had time to take roll and handle your beginning-of-class tasks, transition students to the "before the assessment" activity. Building student agency and meaningful choice into a whole-group rotation can be as simple as adding "would you rather" options throughout the lesson. A "would you rather" choice allows the learner to make key decisions about their path through the lesson to ensure they do not hit barriers to engaging with the learning activities. For example, you can invite students to join a discussion in person or online with a small group of peers to answer the "before the assessment" questions or allow them to reflect on their own in a journal.

A "would you rather" choice allows the learner to make key decisions about their path through the lesson to ensure they do not hit barriers to engaging with the learning activities.

After students have had the time to discuss or reflect, you can transition them to the formative assessment. Ideally, students will have some degree of control over the pace at which they complete the formative assessment. If you are concerned about students finishing early, you can have a "may do" list of items for them to choose from to work on while their peers finish.

When students have completed the formative assessment, they can decide whether they want to join another small-group conversation to answer the "after the assessment" questions or reflect in a journal. This decision might depend on how they feel about their performance. Students who initially joined a discussion may want to follow the formative assessment with a reflection. Learner variability reminds us that not only are students different from each other, but individual learners vary from moment to moment or day to day in terms of their preferences.

Figure 26: Whole-Group Rotation with Exam Wrapper

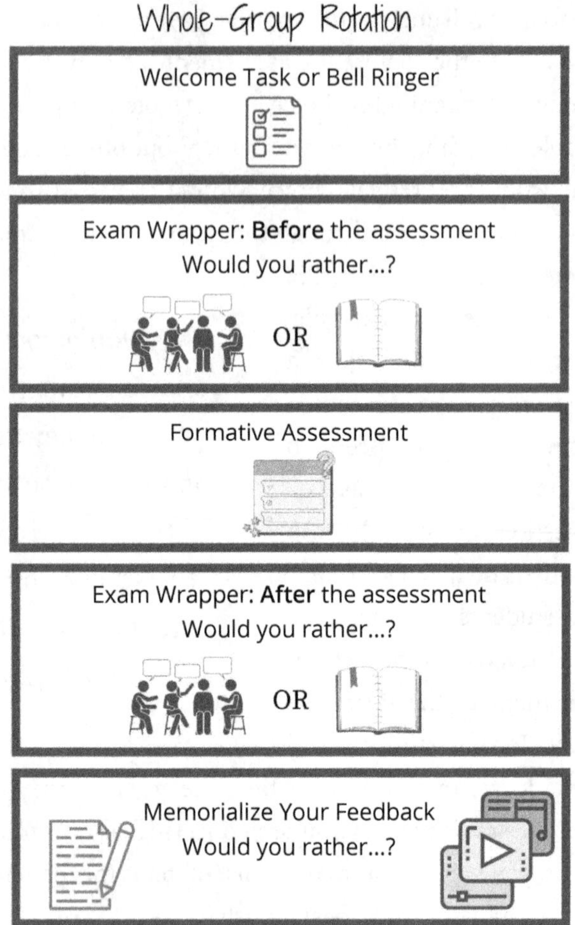

A whole-group rotation is great for a linear, single-day experience with moments in the lesson when it will be beneficial for the students to be working through the same task at the same time, like a formative assessment. Even though a whole-group rotation moves them through the same online and offline learning activities, it is important that we consider where in the lesson we are giving students some degree of control over the pace and path of their learning. We may also want to provide scaffolds, like sentence frames for discussion or reflection, to support learners as they progress through the lesson.

Strategy #3: Memorialize Multiple Means of Feedback

Although it's important to prompt discussions and reflections about learning, it is also beneficial to have a record of student reflections so they can review and notice trends in their learning over time. You can encourage students to memorialize their feedback using a digital portfolio or other compilation of reflections. Each time they reflect on their learning and receive feedback that will grow their expert-learning muscles, they can add an entry reflecting on their learning.

In each entry, students can set goals for their academic and personal growth, celebrate strengths, identify areas in need of development, and summarize feedback they will use in the future. You can use or adapt the choice board in Figure 27 so students can capture their metacognitive process using multiple means of action and expression in their expert-learning portfolios.

Reflections can be captured in an online or offline format, depending on the individual learner's preference. Regardless of the format, the goal is to have students document their learning and revisit this documentation over time to appreciate their growth and construct a more accurate understanding of themselves as learners. Eventually, you may even want to give students a choice about the type of formative assessment strategy they use to demonstrate their learning.

Figure 27: Memorialize Your Feedback Choice Board

Memorialize Your Feedback
After discussing the results of your formative assessment with peers, reflect on your self-assessment process and any/all feedback you received from your peers and your teacher. Summarize what you learned about your strengths and areas where you have the potential for incredible growth using one of the following choices. Once you complete it, add it to your digital portfolio!
Recipe Create a recipe for success! Do you have a specific learning goal (or dish!) you want to work toward? What materials or strategies will you need to build your understanding? What ingredients will you need for this recipe? What steps will you need to follow to make this dish or accomplish this goal?
Dear Diary Write a diary entry sharing your strengths and areas where you will continue to focus your growth. What did you learn about your strengths from this feedback? What did the feedback teach you about the areas where you need to improve? What do you plan to do to act on this feedback? Your diary entry can be handwritten or digital.
Multimedia Use audio or video to record a message to yourself about areas where you can continue to grow your practice as an expert learner. How can you take what you learned to continue to improve? What resources and strategies might you use in the future as you approach a similar task? What support might help you continue improving?

WRAP-UP

It is critical that we use formative assessments *as* learning. When formative assessments are used as compliance tools to "catch" kids in the act of learning or not learning, they don't come close to their potential as drivers of improvement and change. When we transition formative assessments from mini summative assessments to opportunities for expert learning, we shift the cognitive load to students and give them more agency in driving their own success. Ensuring that formative assessments have clear success criteria, facilitate meaningful classroom discussion, and prompt feedback for continued learning and revision is key in universally designed blended learning environments. When formative assessments are used in a teaching-and-learning cycle, a student watches their learning grow over time, as opposed to completing point-in-time assessments that are one and done.

REFLECT AND DISCUSS

1. What form do formative assessments typically take in your class? Would you describe them as assessments *as* learning or *of* learning?
2. What do you do with the data collected during a formative assessment? How often do you make this data available to students?
3. How might building metacognitive routines around formative assessment change the way your students think about them? What impact do you think it would have on the students' understanding of themselves as learners and the class culture around assessment?
4. How might utilizing blended learning models create time and space to employ formative assessment strategies more effectively and consistently?

PUTTING IT INTO PRACTICE

A formative assessment isn't simply a measure of what students know or do not know. It is an invaluable tool for teachers *and* learners to better understand each student's individual progress toward firm goals. They can support students in developing the qualities of an expert learner, helping them to become more resourceful, strategic, and self-aware. Choose one of the strategies outlined in this chapter to transition from formative assessment *of* learning to formative assessment *as* learning in your classroom.

- Strategy #1: Co-create criteria with learners using multiple means
- Strategy #2: Facilitate classroom discussion about formative assessments
- Strategy #3: Memorialize multiple means of feedback

Planning Template 6: Formative Assessment as Learning

What learning objective[s] are you measuring student progress toward with this formative assessment?	
What strategy will you use to collect formative assessment data? • Quiz • Compare and contrast • Create an analogy • Write a summary • Error analysis • 3-2-1 • Other?	
Which strategy for using formative assessment as a metacognitive tool will you use? • Co-create success criteria • Facilitate discussion or reflection with a modified "exam wrapper" • Memorialize multiple means of feedback	
Which blended learning model or strategy will you use to shift control over the pace to students? • Station rotation model • Choice boards • Playlist model • Whole-group rotation model	
How will you encourage students to reflect on what they learned about themselves? • What did they notice about their strengths? • What areas would benefit from further development? • What strategies were effective in helping them prepare for the assessment?	

WORKFLOW SHIFT #7

From Feedback on Finished Products to Feedback during the Process

The Power of Swiff

Katie

When COVID-19 shifted teaching from in person to Zoom, I knew I had to up my game. When we first transitioned, I did what I had seen in a handful of webinars before COVID. I talked. I talked a lot. The more I spoke, the more black screens popped up. I knew there had to be a better way. I created a Google Form with three simple questions and asked for feedback. My form had two qualitative prompts where learners chose their level of agreement on a Likert scale from strongly agree to strongly disagree:

- The presenter was an effective teacher.
- I learned something valuable for my practice from this presentation

And then, the masterstroke was asking a single open-ended question: If there is something I could have done to make your experience more meaningful, please share it here. Use the sentence starter: "It would be cool if . . ."

Being receptive to feedback, I noticed a theme that could be described as "The droning on has got to stop." This included comments such as: "It would be cool if there were time to process," "It would be cool if we had time to interact in the chat," and "It would be cool if there were a time we could ask questions." I was picking up what they were throwing down. I am nothing if not a learner.

I started to provide "chat alerts," two-minute intervals where I paused, took a breath, and encouraged participants to stretch, ask questions, and share their comments in the chat box, in a text with their colleagues, or by posting on social media (you can connect with me and Cat on social media too! @KatieNovakUDL and @Catlin_Tucker!). My "approval ratings" went up, but alas, there was more work to do.

Soon, the feedback shifted to, "Loved the breaks and chats, but it would be cool if there weren't awkward silences." Okay, so Katie Novak staring at everyone from her home office was a little unsettling. Nothing that a little music can't fix. In the spirit of UDL, I used a variety of music clips during chat alerts. I went through periods of the Pointer Sisters, Tina Turner, ABBA, and a cool folk band called Caamp. During the chat alerts, I inserted a timer to support executive function; provided options and choices for people to process, ask questions, etc.; and played some music, encouraging everyone to mute if it was distracting.

The feedback was solid. People were dancing. Life was good. But here's the thing: I was doing all the work, and the music didn't create the type of community and connection I desired. Feedback started shifting to musical requests. I began receiving suggestions like, "It would be cool if you played some country," and "It would be cool if you could play 'September' by Earth, Wind & Fire." Sure, I could embed a couple of videos in the next session. Not solving the problem. Again, I knew I could do better.

I spent excessive time researching artists from around the world and coming up with musical themes for each presentation. Despite all my work, I am 10,000 percent sure that many people never heard a song they truly loved. I mean, as much as I love New Kids on the Block, not everyone jumped out of their seats for "Step by Step." (If you know, you know.)

In December 2020, I presented at a virtual conference and met the brilliant DJ Mr. Swiff. Swiffy is a former radio and nightclub DJ, and now I call him "the" education DJ. His job was to introduce me and then turn off his camera and wait for the next speaker. But, I asked him if he could stay for the short presentation, and during each of the chat alerts, Swiffy took requests. The energy in the presentation changed immediately. He was hired! The feedback in that presentation? "It would be cool if every presentation had a DJ," and "It would be cool if my school had a budget for a DJ for all our meetings!"

Swiff and I started presenting together daily. His presence allowed groups to create their own playlists, which we can share with them when the presentation is over. I'd gone from playing music as a solitary endeavor to teams creating community and connection over their favorite songs.

We start each presentation by setting a timer for a brief period when we encourage requests. People choose the songs they want to hear, and Swiff creates a mix. Every presentation is different and symbolizes the energy and passion of the group. Sometimes, people request songs like the Super Mario Bros. theme song, "Baby Shark," or "The Chicken Dance." We get requests in multiple languages from countries all over the world. I always remind everyone that they have the option to mute but also that every single song is making someone's heart happy.

To me, this journey reflects the power of being open to feedback. Granted, sometimes the feedback I receive is hard to swallow. But the more I ask and make connections, the more I can see my strengths and the areas where I can grow.

As you grow your UDL and blended learning practice, consider how you can ask for feedback and then "Swiff" your practice and take requests. And that doesn't mean that you jump on every piece of feedback you receive, but when you ask—and you listen—you will learn. And sometimes you will need to provide a learning experience even when it's not what students are asking for. I mean, I can't sit by if no one requests "Simply the Best." Everyone needs a little Tina in their lives.

The Research and the Reality: Avoiding the Pitfalls of Feedback

In UDL, we often talk about the importance of choice and voice. Educators are often clear on the importance of choices, but too often, they are the ones who are creating all the options. Students can help to co-create learning experiences if we listen to them and allow them to share their perspectives and their voices. And when we ask, we have to be transparent about what they've shared and how we are going to use their perspective to grow our practice and offer different options.

Providing timely, focused, and actionable feedback is a critical part of forming a partnership with learners where teacher and student work together to share the responsibility for the learning.

Feedback is how students feel seen and supported during the learning process. Providing timely, focused, and actionable feedback is a critical part of forming a partnership with learners where teacher and student work together to share the responsibility for the learning. Unfortunately, feedback is often neglected because class time is used to provide instruction on the "what" and the "how."

Providing timely, focused, and actionable feedback is a critical part of forming a partnership with learners where teacher and student work together to share the responsibility for the learning.

For example, a third-grade math teacher may be focused on a standard that states, "Solve real-world and mathematical problems involving perimeters of polygons, including finding the perimeter given the side lengths, finding an unknown side length, and exhibiting rectangles with the same perimeter and different areas or with the same area and different perimeters." To help students be successful in solving real-world math problems using perimeters of polygons, teachers may provide instruction on shape properties as well as the process of finding the perimeter of polygons using the lengths of the sides. However, it is when students take this instruction and attempt to apply what they learned in practice problems or a performance task that they are likely to encounter a bump, have a question, and need support. Unfortunately, time constraints in traditional classrooms using traditional workflows mean that most teachers do not dedicate equal or greater time to feedback as they do to instruction. Yet feedback during the process allows the teacher to be a facilitator or coach, supporting individual student progress toward mastery of content knowledge and skills.

Traditional approaches to feedback require teachers to collect student work and spend time giving written feedback during their prep periods (when they could be designing dynamic learning experiences) or at home (when they should be relaxing and spending time focusing on self-care). This workflow is time-consuming, often ineffective, and puts all the pressure on the teacher to think critically about student work. Let's take a look at three major challenges posed by giving feedback in this traditional workflow.

- Feedback tends to be infrequent and focuses on minutiae.

- Feedback happens in isolation.
- Feedback is provided on finished products.

Feedback Is Infrequent and Focuses on Minutiae

Even though teachers know feedback is an essential part of the learning process, it is easy to neglect because it is time-consuming to give. Not only do most teachers take feedback home, spending hours of their evenings and weekends leaving comments on student work, but the scope of feedback is far too wide. And, the wider the scope, the more time teachers have to spend with each piece of student work. Most teachers have between 30 and 160 students. That teacher-student ratio means that if a single teacher spends three minutes with each piece of student work (a modest amount by most teachers' standards!), they are investing anywhere from ninety minutes to eight hours of time providing feedback to their students on a single assignment. If that is work that follows a teacher home, it makes sense that teachers would not provide feedback frequently.

Feedback Happens in Isolation

Feedback is an opportunity for a conversation between the teacher and the student. Yet students often complete work in isolation at home, teachers provide feedback in isolation, and that feedback is then delivered to students for them to digest in isolation. This traditional workflow does not create space for a conversation about the student's progress. There are also fewer opportunities in this workflow for students to ask questions or seek additional support if feedback is unclear or they are unsure how to act on it. As a result, some students do not do anything with the feedback they get, which is incredibly frustrating after the time that teachers have invested in the process of providing notes and suggestions.

Feedback Is Provided on Finished Products

Often, feedback is relegated to finished products. Students complete an assignment and submit it for a grade. Teachers review the work, providing comments, suggestions, and corrections. However, at that point, there is zero incentive for students to do anything with the feedback. But if students do not act on feedback then, it will not help them to develop their conceptual understanding or skill sets. By contrast, teachers who provide feedback *as* students work give them the tools and support they need to grow and develop as they progress through an assignment or task. This makes feedback relevant and valuable, because it helps students to create a stronger finished product.

So, not only do the traditional approaches to feedback create mountains of work that teachers haul home, but the time investment does not yield significant results in terms of student growth and development. How do we make feedback more effective and sustainable? How do we get more eyes on student work to ensure the teacher isn't the only person responsible for thinking critically about work and giving students feedback?

John Hattie and Helen Timperley identify feedback as one of the most powerful influences on student achievement and the quality of learning.[1] However, the impact of feedback varies based on the type and timing of that feedback. When done well,

> feedback can lead to increased effort, motivation, or engagement to reduce the discrepancy between the current status and the goal; it can lead to alternative strategies to understand the material; it can confirm for the student that they are correct or incorrect, or how far they have reached the goal; it can indicate that more information is available or needed; it can point to directions that the

1 John Hattie and Helen Timperley, "The Power of Feedback," *Review of Educational Research* 77, no. 1 (March 2007): 81–112.

students could pursue; and, finally, it can lead to restructuring understandings.[2]

In addition to the potential impact on motivation and engagement, it is clear that feedback is critical to students developing a deeper understanding of their strengths, areas they need to improve, and progress toward learning objectives.

Hattie and Timperley identify four levels of feedback. First is feedback on the task: "How well a task is being accomplished or performed, such as distinguishing correct from incorrect answers, acquiring more or different information, and building more surface knowledge." Second is feedback on the process underlying a task. Third is feedback on self-regulation, or the "interplay between commitment, control, and confidence. It addresses the way students monitor, direct, and regulate actions toward the learning goal. It implies autonomy, self-control, self-direction, and self-discipline." Fourth is feedback on the self as a person, which normally takes the form of praise in a classroom. They identify feedback on process and feedback on self-regulation as the most influential types of feedback when it comes to "motivating students and helping them reach deeper levels of understanding and improve their academic performance."[3]

This awareness is critical to cultivating expert learners who are resourceful, strategic, and self-aware. Feedback creates transparency about where students are in their journeys toward mastering specific concepts and skills. With it, students know where to invest more time, energy, and effort to improve. If they find they are not improving or progressing, they can request additional support from the teacher. Feedback during the learning process has the potential

2 John Hattie, Jill Crivelli, Kristin Van Gompel, Patti West-Smith, and Kathryn Wike, "Feedback That Leads to Improvement in Student Essays: Testing the Hypothesis That 'Where to Next' Feedback Is Most Powerful," *Frontiers in Education* 6 (2021), doi.org/10.3389/feduc.2021.645758.

3 Hattie and Timperley, "The Power of Feedback."

to shift students to a more active or proactive position in relation to their progress and learning.

Strategy #1: Model the Power of Feedback

Traditional workflows often present feedback as a one-way street. Teachers spend significant time providing feedback to students, and students—potentially—provide feedback to each other, but they don't often have ongoing opportunities to share feedback about instructional strategies and lessons with their teachers. When you ask learners for feedback, as Katie did in her virtual presentations, you model the power of feedback for improvement. There are numerous ways you can ask students for feedback in your classroom using research-based practices to ensure that the feedback is frequent, collaborative, and formative.

In college classrooms, it is common for learners to provide teacher feedback at the end of the semester. That feedback is on a "finished product." Although the feedback may be helpful for the next group of students, it doesn't do much for the learners who are enrolled in a whole new set of classes. In these classrooms, it would be much more advantageous to the learners for teachers to ask for ongoing feedback throughout the semester and have conversations about how the class is evolving based on that feedback. In their article "A Simple Way for Educators to Get the Feedback They Need," Katie and Lainie Rowell share the power of the sentence starter, "It would be cool if . . ."

> Consider the following feedback scenarios, with and without the scaffold. You ask your class for feedback and get the following:
>
> Scenario 1: This class is too hard. All we do is timed writing which is pointless.

> Scenario 2: It would be cool if we were able to get feedback but not a grade on the timed writing tests so we can go back and revise them to make them better. You say the best writing is rewriting but then we don't have an opportunity to revise in such a short time.
>
> See what happened there? This went from a complaint to high-quality feedback with a suggested solution! When we hear complaints we tend to make assumptions based on our lens of the situation and we often miss the real issue as well as the opportunity to improve.[4]

When we, as educators, provide opportunities for our learners to give us feedback, whether it's on an assessment, during a small-group conversation in a station rotation, or in a survey tool embedded into a playlist, we are creating a culture and climate where feedback is valued.

When we, as educators, provide opportunities for our learners to give us feedback, whether it's on an assessment, during a small-group conversation in a station rotation, or in a survey tool embedded into a playlist, we are creating a culture and climate where feedback is valued.

Strategy #2: Peer-Feedback Choice Board

In a learning community, all members should play a role in providing thoughtful and substantive feedback, yet students are not always sure how to give kind and specific feedback. They need explicit

4 Katie Novak and Lainie Rowell, "A Simple Way for Educators to Get the Feedback They Need," *Inspired Ideas*, November 22, 2021, medium.com/inspired-ideas-prek-12/a-simple-way-for-educators-to-get-the-feedback-they-need-559e9c6bc60.

instruction and practice giving peer feedback if it is going to be valuable and constructive.

Peer feedback is most effective when it is focused and comes with clear guidelines. A choice board, like the one in Figure 28, can provide students with a sense of agency as they attempt to give each other focused and substantive feedback on an assignment. Building student agency into the peer-feedback process removes barriers and encourages students to provide feedback through a specific lens. Based on what a student sees in the work they are reviewing, they may be drawn to one option on the choice board over another.

Figure 28: Peer-Feedback Choice Board

Peer-Feedback Choice Board	
Directions: Select TWO prompts from the peer-feedback choice board to provide your classmate with specific, meaningful, and kind feedback. Capture your feedback in the space below the choice board!	
Greatest Strength Identify the strongest aspect of this assignment. What specifically was strong? Why do you think this element was particularly powerful or well done? How did this element positively impact the overall quality of this work?	**Tiny Tweaks** Identify one aspect of this assignment that would benefit from a minor adjustment, modification, or tweak. What would you suggest the student rework or reimagine? How would reworking this element impact the overall quality of this work? Do you have specific recommendations for how they might improve this aspect of their work?

Celebrate Surprises As you reviewed this assignment, what surprised you about this student's work? Was there an aspect of their work that was unexpected, original, outside-of-the-box, engaging, or thought-provoking? Describe why you liked this aspect of their work.	**Hungry for More** Identify a part of this assignment that needs further development. What would you have enjoyed knowing more about or having more information on? Where could more detail and development have strengthened this? Can you identify the specific places in this assignment where the student should spend time digging deeper?
Mind Blown Identify something in this assignment that you loved and had not considered as you completed your work. Is there a great idea or approach that this student used to complete this assignment that you would like to incorporate into your work? Why did you like this element of their draft? How can you incorporate this idea or approach into your work?	**Clarifying Confusion** As you reviewed this assignment, was there anything unclear, confusing, or that left you wondering? Is there an aspect of this draft that you would like clarity on or more specifics about? Were any of the steps or statements unclear? Can you identify specific elements of this assignment that would benefit from clearer language or more explanation?
Choice Board Selection Write your feedback below. Please be specific and kind.	
Title of Feedback Prompt #1:	
Title of Feedback Prompt #2:	

Teachers working with younger students or second-language learners can create a choice board with built-in sentence frames to provide students with additional support as they give each other focused feedback. For example, under the box labeled "Greatest Strength," teachers could include a series of fill-in-the-blank statements:

- "The strongest part of this draft was ________."
- "I thought _______ was done well."
- "I really liked _____."

Each option in the choice board could be composed of fill-in-the-blank statements for younger students or students who need additional scaffolds to complete the activity.

Additionally, teachers can give students options for how they communicate feedback—in writing, a short video, or an audio recording—to ensure they are able to express their thinking effectively.

Strategy #3: Peer Feedback with Rubrics

Rubrics are like road maps. They provide clarity about the learning objectives and goals that students are working toward. When we provide rubrics at the start of an assignment, task, or project that will be assessed using a rubric, we demystify the grading process and help students understand what they need to do to be successful. This transparency can make a task less daunting, provide an incentive for continuing to refine and develop work, and encourage students to ask questions or seek support if they are unsure what a criterion on the rubric is asking them to do.

If teachers create a standards-aligned rubric that includes descriptions of what the individual skills "look like" on a scale of 1 (beginning) to 4 (mastery), students can use a modified version of that rubric to give each other peer feedback, as in Figure 29. Teachers can add a column to their rubric that encourages students to provide a brief explanation for each score they give their partner.

Structuring peer feedback this way has the added benefit of helping students become familiar with the rubric that the teacher will use to assess their finished products. As they read the language of the rubric and evaluate their peer's work, they may realize that aspects of their own work are absent or need development and revision.

Figure 29: Peer Feedback with Rubrics

Peer Review

Directions: Please use this rubric to assess your partner's argumentative writing. Circle the score you would give each element of this piece of writing and explain your reasoning.

- Why did you give this work the score you did on each criterion?
- What did you notice in the work that aligned with the level of mastery?
- How might this element be improved or developed?

Criteria	1. Beginning	2. Developing	3. Proficient	4. Mastery	Peer Review
Claim	Claim is unclear. No clear reasons are given.	Claim is clear, but the reasons are unclear, absent, or incomplete.	Claim and reasons are clearly stated.	Claim is clearly stated and the reasons are strong.	
Evidence	Central claim is not supported. No evidence provided.	Attempts to support the central claim and reasons with facts, but information is unclear, inaccurate, or lacks citations.	Supports the central claim and reasons with fact, necessary details, and citations.	Supports the central claim and reasons with strong facts, thorough details, and accurate citations.	
Explanation	Contains little to no explanation or analysis of the information presented.	Attempts to explain and analyze the information, but the explanation is unclear or inaccurate.	Clearly explains and analyzes most of the information presented.	Clearly, concisely, and thoroughly explains and analyzes the information presented.	

Peer feedback aims to engage the learning community in the process of thinking about the work they are doing and how they are supporting each other. These peer-feedback activities position students at the center of the learning and require that *they* think critically about each other's work. Peer-feedback routines also lighten the load for teachers because they are no longer the only source of specific and substantive feedback in the classroom.

Strategy #4: Real-Time Feedback

Time is the biggest obstacle to providing consistent and timely feedback. Teachers never have enough time. However, research suggests that students want feedback that is "specific, useful, and timely" and "relative to the criteria or standards they are assessed against."[5] So, to make feedback useful and timely, we have to find ways to shift the task of giving it into the classroom and avoid taking it home. As teachers explore blended learning models and lean on video and other multimedia resources to move the transfer of information online, they can shift from their role as expert at the front of the room to facilitator providing focused, actionable feedback on work in progress.

When students are completing a task that is a process, meaning that there are multiple steps in a task or it is likely to take them more than a single sitting to complete, they will benefit from feedback *as* they work. This shifts the focus from the product to the process, communicating to students that our priority is on supporting their continued improvement and reinforces a growth mindset.

Teachers can use blended learning models to create time to give feedback in the classroom instead of taking it home. For example, teachers using the station rotation model can dedicate their teacher-led station to real-time feedback, as pictured in Figure 30.

5 John Hattie et al., "Feedback That Leads to Improvement in Student Essays."

Figure 30: Real-Time Feedback Station

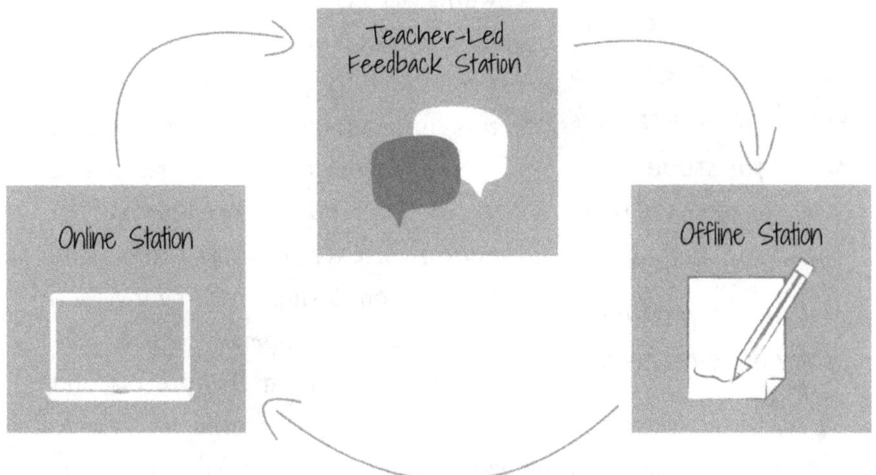

At the station, students have time to continue working on a writing assignment, multi-step project, or performance task, while the teacher jumps into and out of digital documents or physically carousels around the group to look at offline work and provide focused feedback. This gives students class time to make progress on the assignment while allowing the teacher to give feedback during class.

Using the teacher-led station in a station rotation lesson to provide students with feedback as they work necessitates that teachers limit the scope of their feedback. A teacher may have twenty to twenty-five minutes to provide feedback to six to eight students. That translates into approximately three minutes per work sample. So, it is important to identify which element of the assignment you are going to focus on in advance of the real-time feedback session and explicitly tell students what to expect in terms of the feedback. If students are working on a piece of writing, you might identify one aspect of the writing process to provide feedback on in a given session. However, you will not have time to fix all of a student's grammatical errors, so it's important to make that clear. Instead, suggest they use Grammarly to check their mechanics or exchange papers

Real-time feedback lightens the teacher's workload and creates space for students to ask questions if they are unsure how to act on the feedback they have received.

with a partner for additional feedback. By contrast, if your students are working through the parts of a performance task in math class or a multimedia project in history, you can select one step in that process or one aspect of the performance task or project to provide feedback on during this time together. As Hattie and Timperley suggest, providing feedback on the process and strategies being employed is likely to have the biggest impact on helping students develop a deeper understanding of key concepts and proficiency in applying specific skills.

Real-time feedback lightens the teacher's workload and creates space for students to ask questions if they are unsure how to act on the feedback they have received. These feedback sessions help students feel supported in their work and, as a result, help them develop higher levels of self-efficacy over time. Building this confidence is critical to cultivating expert learners.

Strategy #5: Read Feedback and Reflect

Feedback should aid students in understanding themselves as learners. However, it is helpful if students are asked to regularly reflect on their feedback. A read-and-reflect routine accomplishes a couple of important objectives. First, it requires that students spend time reading the feedback they have received from their classmates or their teacher. Second, the reflection encourages them to think about what they are learning about themselves as a result of that feedback. What are their areas of strength? What areas do they need to spend more time and energy developing, improving, or practicing? Where do they see growth? How do they plan to act on that feedback?

Hattie and Timperley describe a feedback model that is built on three central questions.

- Where am I going?
- How am I going?
- Where to next?[6]

Where Am I Going?

This first question refers to the "learning goals related to the task or performance." Teachers must make sure students understand what they are working toward by making the learning goals clear at the start of an assignment. Providing a rubric that shows exactly how you plan to assess those learning goals is helpful in providing students with a road map to follow as they work.

How Am I Going?

This second question requires that the teacher, a classmate, or the student themself provides "information relative to a task or performance goal, often in relation to some expected standard, to prior performance, and/or to success or failure on a specific part of the task."[7] Teachers can provide this type of feedback during a real-time feedback station or by conferencing with individual students about their progress on an assignment or task. Other students in the class can provide this type of feedback using the peer-feedback rubric described in strategy #2. Finally, students can think critically about their own work, compare it to previous work samples, complete a self-assessment using the rubric, and reflect on their performance.

Where to Next?

This question should provide students with a path forward, "providing information that leads to greater possibilities for

6 Hattie and Timperley, "The Power of Feedback."

7 Ibid.

Figure 31: Read Feedback and Reflect Form

<table>
<tr><th colspan="2">Read Feedback + Reflect</th></tr>
<tr><td colspan="2">Directions: Read the feedback you have received. Reflect on what you learned about yourself, your work, and what you need to do next to continue making progress.</td></tr>
<tr><td>Who provided you with feedback?</td><td></td></tr>
<tr><td>Areas of strength:
• What are your areas of strength?
• What strategies are you using that are working well?</td><td></td></tr>
<tr><td>Areas in need of improvement:
• What aspects of your work need further development or improvement?
• Is there a strategy, skill, or concept you need to spend more time and energy developing, improving, or practicing?
• Is there an area of weakness that you would like more support to improve? What type of support do you think would be most useful?</td><td></td></tr>
<tr><td>Areas of growth:
• As you reflect on the feedback you received, where do you see growth?
• What aspects of your work demonstrate improvement from earlier work?</td><td></td></tr>
<tr><td>Action plan: Where to next?
• How will you act on the feedback you received?
• What areas of this assignment will you rework and/or develop?
• What new strategies will you try?
• What specific steps do you plan to take to improve this assignment?
• What goal do you have for yourself as you continue working with this assignment?</td><td></td></tr>
</table>

learning. These may include enhanced challenges, more self-regulation over the learning process, greater fluency and automaticity, more strategies and processes to work on the tasks, deeper understanding, and more information about what is and what is not understood."[8] When asking students to reflect on feedback they have received from a teacher or a peer, we should encourage them to articulate the answer to the "where to next" question in their reflections. How will they act on the feedback they have received? Thinking through this final question can provide clarity about what they need to do to continue making progress and improving. It can also help them to appreciate the value of the feedback they have received.

Figure 32: WOW Reflection Slide Deck

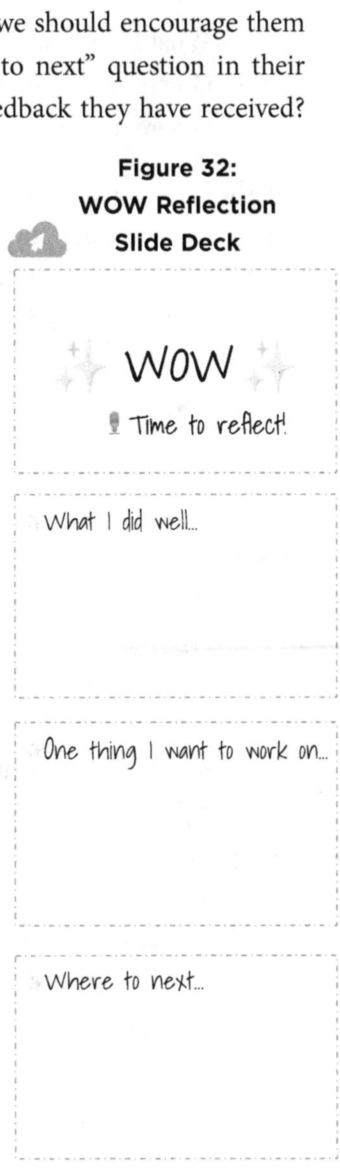
WOW
Time to reflect!
What I did well...
One thing I want to work on...
Where to next...

You can encourage students to reflect more deeply by providing them with a structure, as shown in Figure 31. A reflection form can help students to think about their strengths, areas in need of improvement, areas of growth, and next steps.

Developing a reflective practice is something we should encourage in learners of all ages. Elementary teachers who want to help younger students learn to reflect on feedback can create a simplified version of this read-and-reflect routine. Instead of a digital document, which may be challenging for younger learners to navigate, teachers can create a WOW

8 Ibid.

digital slide deck that can be completed online or printed for offline use, as pictured in Figure 32. A simple acronym, like WOW, can keep the scope of reflection manageable, while still encouraging students to think about the feedback and reflect on the following aspects of their work:

- **W**hat I did well
- **O**ne thing I want to work on
- **W**here to next?

The beauty of a digital slide deck is that students can use the accessibility features inside the deck. They can also use the voice-typing tool to compose typed responses, insert a video recording, or take pictures of drawings and insert them into each slide.

Strategy #6: Leveraging Media for Feedback

Research suggests that using media beyond text comments positively impacts a student's perception of the quality of feedback. Students who receive audio feedback when learning online perceived that feedback as more thorough, detailed, and motivating than text-based feedback.[9] Students also reported being more motivated by audio and video feedback because it was clear and felt personalized.[10] Interestingly, teachers also reported higher levels of engagement when giving video and audio feedback.

For teachers working with students online or on a hybrid schedule—where they learn, in part, asynchronously from home—using video and audio comments can also help build relationships, connecting teacher and learner despite the asynchronous nature of

9 S. Voelkel and L. V. Mello, "Audio Feedback—Better Feedback?," *Bioscience Education* 22, no. 1: 16–30.

10 M. Henderson and M. Phillips, "Video-Based Feedback on Student Assessment: Scarily Personal," *Australasian Journal of Educational Technology* 31, no. 1.

online work. Feedback here is likely to contain more depth than written comments because students benefit from seeing facial expressions and hearing the teacher's tone of voice. This can lead to increased understanding of the feedback and improved success acting on the feedback. As with all things in UDL, it is important to give students a choice. For example, you could use a choice board, like the one in Figure 33, with learners when they submit a draft of a product they are working on to allow them to choose which type of feedback works best for them.

Figure 33: Choose Your Feedback Format

Your Choice: What Type of Feedback Would You Like?	
Written Feedback Please send me written feedback on my assignment. 	**Audio Feedback** Please send me an audio file with feedback on my assignment because it will be helpful for me to hear your voice.
Video Feedback Please send me a video file with feedback on my assignment because it will be helpful for me to see your face and hear your voice.	**Video Screen Share** Please send me a video file where you project my assignment and walk me through it while you give your feedback because it will be helpful for me to see your face and hear your voice while also seeing my work.

WRAP-UP

Feedback is one of the most powerful tools teachers have in their teaching tool belts for guiding learners toward mastery. Without feedback, students do not have a clear sense of what they are doing well, what they need to focus on, and what they can do to improve.

Despite the power of timely and actionable feedback, it is easy to neglect. Providing feedback is time-consuming and often takes a back seat to other aspects of our work. It's critical that we find ways to give feedback that are sustainable and effective. Teachers can help students to give each other meaningful peer feedback, use blended learning models to pull real-time feedback into the classroom, and encourage students to reflect on the feedback they receive to understand their strengths and weaknesses.

REFLECT AND DISCUSS

1. Feedback is often infrequent, isolated, and provided on final products. How do your own feedback practices compare?
2. What strategy can you use to collect feedback regularly from your students? How might regularly collecting feedback from your students impact your class culture?
3. How can you shift your practice to ask students for feedback that is frequent, collaborative, and formative to model the importance of effective feedback practices and build student ownership of the learning environment?
4. How can the strategies in this chapter help you to build a culture where peer feedback is valuable and meaningful to learners?
5. If you were given an option to receive feedback on your own lesson design (e.g., written, audio, video, or video with a screen recording), what would you choose and why?

PUTTING IT INTO PRACTICE

This chapter highlighted six strategies for shifting feedback workflows from teacher to student. Review the following strategies and make a commitment to implementing one of the shifts into your classroom in the next week. As you transition, be sure to ask for feedback on how the shifts impact student ownership and engagement in the learning process.

- Strategy #1: Model the power of feedback
- Strategy #2: Peer-feedback choice board
- Strategy #3: Peer feedback with rubrics
- Strategy #4: Real-time feedback
- Strategy #5: Read feedback and reflect
- Strategy #6: Leveraging media for feedback

Planning Template 7: Feedback during the Process

What strategy will you use to shift feedback into the classroom? • Model the power of feedback • Peer-feedback choice board • Peer feedback with rubrics • Real-time feedback • Read feedback and reflect • Leveraging audio or video for feedback	
What element or aspect of the assignment will feedback focus on?	
Who will give feedback—you or your students? • If students are giving each other feedback, what scaffolds or supports will they need to ensure that feedback is substantive, constructive, and respectful?	
Which blended learning model or strategy will you use to shift feedback in the classroom? • Station rotation model • Choice boards • Playlist model • Whole-group rotation model	
How will you encourage students to reflect on what they learned about themselves from the feedback they received? • What did they notice about their strengths? • What areas would benefit from further development? • Where do they need additional instruction or support?	

WORKFLOW SHIFT #8

From Teacher Assessment to Self-Assessment

Death by a Thousand "Ums"

Catlin

In 2013, I delivered my first big keynote at the Computer-Using Educators (CUE) Conference in Palm Springs. The conference organizers asked if I would kick off the event as the opening keynote. I was flattered to be asked—and totally terrified. Sir Ken Robinson was the headline keynote, and seeing my face alongside his on the promotional materials shared on social media leading up to the event was surreal. As a typical type A, I dealt with my anxiety about the event by taking control of the one thing I could control: my preparation. I sketched an outline of my talk, put together a multimedia PowerPoint presentation, then drafted a script of my keynote. I did not intend to memorize my talk, but I wanted to think through the content and the transitions in detail. Once I was happy with the script, I recorded an audio file on my phone and listened to it while walking my dog, running errands, and finally while flying from San Francisco to Palm Springs.

After being introduced, I mounted the stage with my Janet Jackson microphone tucked around my ear, my trusty clicker in hand, and butterflies in my stomach. It only took a minute or two for me to transition from feeling nervous and awkward on stage to hitting my stride and relaxing into the talk I had spent weeks preparing. The audience laughed at my jokes about the realities of teaching. They made affirming noises as I talked about how to integrate technology into classrooms to shift students to the center of the learning experience. And, at the end, they erupted in applause. I felt like I had done a good job.

When I returned home, I remember talking to my parents on the phone. They had watched my keynote, which had been published on YouTube. My dad, who manages to say a lot without using many words, said, "You did well. You'll need to work on all those 'ums.'" I was crestfallen. Had I said "um" a lot? Did I dare watch my keynote to see if he was correct?

I bit the bullet and decided to watch it. I figured if I was going to learn from the experience, I should take a cue from professional football players and watch the film! Agh. It was painful. Yes, the content of my keynote was strong, but I did say "um" quite a bit. Each time it came out of my mouth, I cringed a little. I'd have to work on slowing down and being aware of leaning on filler words to give my brain time to catch up with my mouth. I noticed that my dangling earrings were making a rhythmic clicking noise against my Janet Jackson microphone. Repetitive noises drive me nuts, so my skin was crawling by the ten-minute mark. Note to self: Wear studs when delivering a keynote. Finally, I realized that I am a big gesticulator and have a tendency to throw my hands around willy-nilly when I speak. Sometimes it worked to emphasize a point, and sometimes it distracted from what I was saying. I knew controlling my tendency to gesticulate would be another area I needed to work on in advance of future keynotes.

Watching myself on film was not a particularly enjoyable experience. I had to face the aspects of my performance that did not work well, but I also learned a great deal about myself as a public speaker. I could appreciate that my humor, the multimedia elements of my presentation, and my content were engaging, which was clear from the moments when the camera captured clips of the audience. I also had a list of things to work on before I set foot on another stage.

As tough as it is to watch myself on stage speaking, I've made a habit of following any keynote that is recorded with a self-assessment. I watch the recording, and I make note of what went well and what I need to work to improve the next time I speak in front of a group. It is this process of sitting down to analyze each keynote video that has helped me to develop as a public speaker over time. Similarly, we must help our students engage in the same self-assessment process to develop their metacognitive muscles and better understand themselves as learners. It is only then that we will be successful in cultivating expert learners capable of making informed decisions about their learning and accessing the support they need as they progress down their personalized learning paths.

The Research and Reality: The Value of Self-Assessment

Self-assessment is a "reflective process where students use criteria to evaluate their performance and determine how to improve."[1] It's designed to be formative in nature, helping students improve their current and future performance. Learning how to look at their work and comparing it with exemplars and a clear set of success criteria can positively impact student motivation, metacognition, and the ability to self-regulate, all of which are critical to expert learners.[2]

1 Amy Siegesmund, "Using Self-Assessment to Develop Metacognition and Self-Regulated Learners," *FEMS Microbiology Letters* 364, no. 11, doi.org/10.1093/femsle/fnx096.

2 Amy Siegesmund, "Increasing Student Metacognition and Learning through Classroom-Based Learning Communities and Self-Assessment," *Journal of Microbiology & Biology Education* 17, no. 2 (May 2016): 204–14.

Metacognition, or "a high level of thinking that involves control over one's cognitive processes engaged in learning" is critical for self-assessment.[3]

Self-assessment positively impacts student motivation, because it fosters the basic psychological needs of autonomy and competence identified as essential to human motivation by Richard Ryan and Edward Deci's self-determination theory. When students regularly assess their work, they enjoy autonomy, or independence and ownership of their actions. They begin to appreciate that they have control over their learning and academic performance. They can make decisions and employ specific strategies that can directly impact their experience in positive ways. They are no longer passive receivers of assignments and grades; rather, they have opportunities to assess and reflect on their work to continually improve it. As a result, they develop higher levels of competence, or confidence in their ability to develop, grow, and achieve mastery.[4] Together, the autonomy and competence involved in self-assessment can positively impact our students' motivation.

As students engage in regular self-assessment activities, they develop the ability to regulate cognition by evaluating the effectiveness of the strategies they've employed and gauge their performance against clear success criteria for a particular task. Metacognition is a critical driver of expert learning.

Finally, self-assessment improves overall self-regulation skills, which are critical to success in a blended learning environment, where students enjoy more autonomy and agency over their experience. Self-regulation is a broad term that encompasses a person's ability to stay attentive to tasks and control their own behavior to

---

3 Athanasia Chatzipanteli, Vasilis Grammatikopoulos, and Athanasios Gregoriadis, "Development and Evaluation of Metacognition in Early Childhood Education," *Early Child Development and Care* 184, no. 8: 1223–32.

4 R. Ryan and E. Deci, "Intrinsic and Extrinsic Motivation from a Self-Determination Theory Perspective: Definitions, Theory, Practices, and Future Directions," *Contemporary Educational Psychology* 61, doi.org/10.1016/j.cedpsych.2020.101860.

accomplish a specific outcome.[5] As a result, it is critical that we prepare students with the necessary "tools they need to focus and pay attention, keep their emotions in check, adjust to change, or handle the frustration that is sometimes a part of interacting with others or learning something new."[6] Even young learners benefit from explicit instruction and support aimed at developing their self-regulation skills. The development of these skills is linked to improved academic performance but also to future success beyond school.[7]

Even though the value of self-assessment is clear in the research, it can be easy to neglect, because—like any skill—it takes time, scaffolding, and practice to master. Students may initially struggle to sit with their work, analyze how it is similar to or different from strong examples, and evaluate their content knowledge and skill set using standard-aligned rubrics and success criteria. This is a cognitively demanding exercise.

However, a consistent routine of self-assessment over time can help learners to develop both their metacognitive muscles and a more comprehensive understanding of themselves as learners. As students develop a deeper awareness of their skills and abilities as learners, they are more likely to make decisions and select learning paths that will help them to continue to grow and develop as learners. They are also more likely to advocate for their specific needs, requesting additional support and asking questions.

---

5 Janelle J. Montroy et al., "The Development of Self-Regulation across Early Childhood," *Developmental Psychology* 52, no. 11 (November 2016): 1744–62.

6 Nina Parrish, "How to Teach Self-Regulation," George Lucas Educational Foundation, August 22, 2018, edutopia.org/article/how-teach-self-regulation.

7 Montroy et al., "The Development of Self-Regulation across Early Childhood."

Strategy #1: Exemplars, Vocabulary, and Success Criteria

To successfully engage in self-assessment, students need three things—exemplars, vocabulary, and clear success criteria![8] Exemplars are strong examples of the work students are creating. So, if your students are writing a lab report or designing a multimedia slide deck, they will benefit from seeing strong examples to identify what those examples have in common. It's helpful to strategically pair or group students for the exercise of analyzing a few strong examples of the work they are doing. They are more likely to be effective at identifying the essential elements and strengths present in these examples if they are able to collaborate with their peers and engage in discussion about what they are noticing in the exemplars. You may want to provide a template, like the one in Figure 34, to guide these conversations and encourage students to document what they are learning so they can strengthen and improve their own work.

You can use examples from previous students, ask other teachers in your department or on social media, gather examples of work online, or create exemplars for students to reference. We suggest you save examples of strong student work so you don't have to spend time generating exemplars. However, we know this isn't possible when you are new to the teaching profession, teaching a new class, or are asking students to complete a task or project that you have never assigned before. If you do have to invest the time to create your own exemplars, make a mental note to identify strong examples to use in the future from the final projects or products that you assess.

Once students have a clear understanding of what strong examples of this work look like, what characteristics they have in common, and what elements are included, then you will want

8 Emelina Minero, "4 Steps of Student Self-Assessment," George Lucas Educational Foundation, October 4, 2016, edutopia.org/practice/mastering-self-assessment-deepening-independent-learning-through-arts.

to identify key vocabulary they will need to successfully conduct their self-assessments. Each subject area has domain- and academic-specific vocabulary that may be unfamiliar to students. If you spend time helping students build their vocabularies, their self-assessments (as well as their insight into their own work) will be stronger. You may want to copy, modify, and use the Frayer Model template (Figure 35), to encourage pairs or small groups of students to analyze unfamiliar vocabulary. You can also provide a vocabulary-attainment choice board composed of a variety of activities designed to help them practice using the words.

Figure 34: Analyzing Exemplars Template

Analyzing Exemplars		
Exemplars	**Essential Elements** What elements do you notice in this exemplar?	**Strengths** What do you think is strong about this piece?
Exemplar #1		
Exemplar #2		
Exemplar #3		

Reflection	
What do all three exemplars have in common?	
What did you learn about analyzing these exemplars that you believe will help you to be successful on this assignment, task, or project?	
What questions do you have about this assignment, task, or project?	

Figure 35: Vocabulary Development

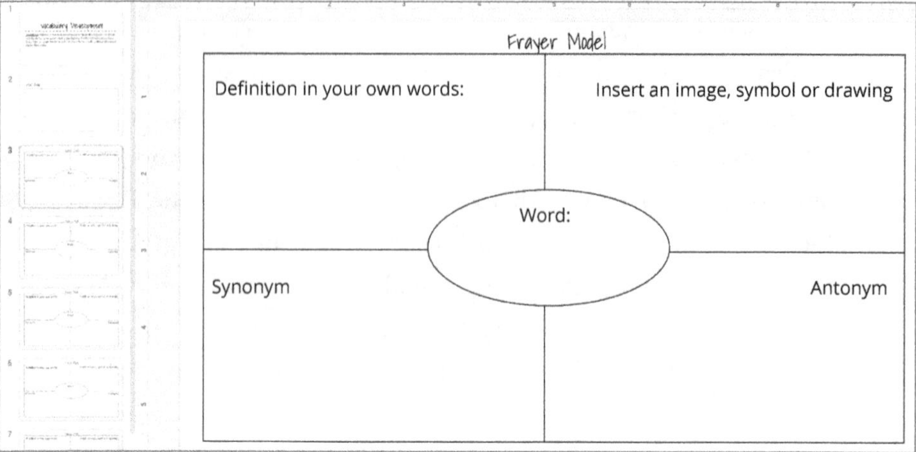

You can provide students agency by giving them a word bank of key vocabulary and asking them to select three to five words that they want to focus on for this exercise. That way, they can choose to learn the words *they* think will be most beneficial to focus on. Allowing students to select their words from a word bank also allows for a degree of personalization. If you want to differentiate this experience, you can provide groups with additional support and scaffolds by pulling this activity into a teacher-led station where you can guide students, provide additional resources, and answer questions.

Finally, students need to understand what success looks like on this particular assignment, task, or project. Ideally, teachers will create standard-aligned rubrics *with* students to ensure they understand the intended outcomes in advance of beginning the task. Rubrics serve as helpful guides and road maps for learners if they are simple and clear. To design an effective rubric, teachers and learners need to understand what the work *should* demonstrate in terms of content knowledge and skill set. Often, students are given assignments without clear learning outcomes or success criteria, which is a bit like going on a road trip without knowing your destination. It's hard to arrive at the Grand Canyon if you didn't know that's where you were headed!

The best rubrics use student-friendly language to describe what learning looks like at different levels of mastery, so students don't have to guess what a three out of four means or what "proficient" looks like. It is easy to create rubrics with a simple number scale or labels like "beginning, developing, proficient, and mastery." However, if we don't take the time to describe what each level or number actually looks like, the rubric is unlikely to guide students in improving their work.

If you are asking students to analyze exemplars, you can have them work collaboratively in small groups to identify one clear element, concept, or skill evident in the exemplars. Then they can work together to describe what they think that element would look like at different levels of mastery using a simple rubric. The digital slide deck pictured in Figure 36 is designed to allow each group to take a slide; build out the rubric for their chosen element, concept, or skill; and see each other's work. This exercise requires critical thinking and builds metacognitive awareness. The more time students spend working to generate their own success criteria, the more successful they will be at engaging in self-assessment and improving their work.

Figure 36: Student-Designed Success Criteria

Success Criteria:

Beginning 1	Developing 2	Proficient 3	Mastery 4

If students have opportunities to analyze strong examples, develop the necessary vocabulary, and access clear success criteria, they'll be more successful in engaging in thoughtful self-assessment.

Strategy #2: Reflective Journaling, Podcasting, or Blogging

Reflection is a critical component of the learning process and an important part of any self-assessment activity. We don't want students to simply assess their work using a rubric or set of success criteria, we want them to think deeply about what they learned about themselves from this self-assessment. Asking students to follow every self-assessment with a reflection can help them to appreciate what they are learning as a result of this process. These reflections are also a wonderful way to document growth over time.

You can offer students a variety of options for how they capture their reflections. Some students might enjoy writing in a traditional journal or drawing sketchnotes to capture their reflections. Others might enjoy producing a podcast about their learning journey or publishing audio recordings detailing their reflections following specific assignments. Still others might enjoy creating a learning blog where they pull together documentation of their learning with written reflections. Giving students agency over the format of their reflections is likely to yield stronger, more meaningful reflections. You can copy the post-self-assessment reflection choice board in Figure 37 to allow students to select the strategy they want to use to capture their reflections. Regardless of the format they select, you should provide them with a list of questions to guide their reflections.

Figure 37: Self-Assess Then Reflect Choice Board

Consider the following questions as you complete your post-self-assessment reflection:

- What aspects of your work were particularly strong?
- What strategies did you use that worked well?
- What was missing from your work?
- Where would your work benefit from further depth, detail, or development?
- What might you do differently in the future?
- Where are you seeing growth in your work?
- Are there areas where you feel like you need additional instruction or support?

The goal of pairing a reflective practice with self-assessment is to encourage students to think more deeply about what they learned during the self-assessment process. That way, they can act on what they learned to continually improve and feel agency over their learning.

Strategy #3: Ongoing Self-Assessment Routine

If students are going to develop as learners, they need to track their progress, reflect on their specific skills, and identify areas that need more time, attention, and improvement.

We want students to take an active role not only in their learning but also in the assessment of their progress as learners. Yet students are rarely asked to *think* about their learning or monitor their progress through ongoing self-assessment. Building a consistent self-assessment practice into your classroom can help students to:

1. Appreciate the impact of the work they are doing on their content knowledge and skills. They will also understand what standards and skills specific assignments and tasks are targeting, so they don't mentally file items as "busy work" because they do not understand the purpose or value of them.
2. Begin to recognize the areas where they are making strides and growing as well as the areas where they may be stagnating and need additional support. This translates into learners who are able to advocate for themselves by requesting additional help.
3. Get comfortable thinking about their learning and develop confidence in their ability to improve their skills through hard work and practice, reinforcing a growth mindset!

Figure 38 is a template for an ongoing-self-assessment form that you can copy, modify, and use with your students. There are four sections to the ongoing-self-assessment document. First, there is a section for the target standards or skills associated with a unit of study or a learning cycle. It's important that these be written in student-friendly language so learners understand what they are being asked to do. You can encourage groups of students to work collaboratively to read each standard, discuss its meaning, and rewrite it in language that makes sense to them. This can be done as part of a station rotation or whole-group rotation lesson.

The second section is where students insert the name of the assignment they have chosen to assess. This allows the student to decide which piece of work they want to spend time assessing. If you are teaching younger students, you can identify the specific

Figure 38: Ongoing-Self-Assessment Document

<table>
<tr><th colspan="2">Ongoing-Self-Assessment Document</th></tr>
<tr><td colspan="2">Think about the work you have completed this week. Select a specific piece of work to analyze and reflect on in-depth.
• Identify the skill or standard to which this particular piece of work aligns.
• What is the title of the assignment you are assessing? Provide a link to online work or insert a photo of offline work.
• Evaluate your work and give yourself a score based on where you think you are in relation to mastering this skill/standard.
• Explain your self-evaluation score.</td></tr>
<tr><td>Standard/Skill</td><td></td></tr>
<tr><td>Title of the Assignment and Documentation
(Include a link or insert an image)</td><td></td></tr>
<tr><td>Self-Assessment Score (1-4)
1 = Beginning...I still need support.
2 = Developing...I'm getting the hang of this.
3 = Proficient...I got this.
4 = Mastery...I'm ready for the next challenge.</td><td></td></tr>
<tr><td>Explanation/Reflection
• Why did you give yourself a particular score?
• What details in your work support the self-evaluation score you assigned to this piece?
• What does this piece show about your strengths as a student?
• What aspects of this skill or standard are you still working on or struggling with?
• What specific support would help you continue to develop this skill?</td><td></td></tr>
</table>

assignment, skill, or behavior you want them to assess. Then they can link to the work if it lives online or include a photo so you can easily reference the work they are assessing.

The third section is for their self-assessment score. We've included a simple four-point mastery scale that includes the four stages of beginning, developing, proficient, and mastery; however, if you work with younger learners, you may want to replace the number scale with emojis or other symbols to simplify the self-assessment process.

Finally, the fourth section encourages students to reflect on the score they gave themselves, explaining what aspects of their work support their self-assessment score. You can invite students to complete the reflection on this document, record an audio explanation, or capture a short video explaining their self-assessment score. The goal of the reflection is to encourage students to support or justify their self-assessment score using details from their work.

Strategy #4: Showcasing Growth with Student Portfolios

Learning is a dynamic process that requires active engagement. Unfortunately, many students have gotten comfortable in their roles as passive observers, or consumers, in the classroom. Yes, that is a less cognitively and socially taxing role, but it is not nearly as interesting or engaging. An effective way to shift our students' thinking about their role in the classroom is to teach them how to treat their learning like they are making a documentary. The beauty of this mindset is that it demands that students capture, reflect on, and share their learning. Digital multimedia portfolios are a fabulous way to encourage students to document and reflect on their learning!

Our friend George Couros distinguishes between two types of portfolios: a learning portfolio and a showcase portfolio.[9] In a learning portfolio, a student consistently monitors their progress. For example, if you were to use a learning portfolio in your classroom, students could share all assessments, progress, and reflections on a consistent schedule. In a showcase portfolio, students post the work they are most proud of to highlight, or showcase, their learning. He notes, "What is beautiful in using a blog as a portfolio is that you do not have to choose; you can do both." We believe the same is true for all student portfolios.

Multimedia documentation can be integrated into a digital portfolio to *show* the student's work and growth over time. Students can use their devices to:

- Take photos of work in progress, experiments, labs, art projects, etc.
- Capture a progression or slow change with a timelapse.
- Record videos of works in progress, presentations, or demonstrations.
- Use audio capture to record notes, realizations, or document interviews.

As students develop their own learning portfolios and showcase their most exemplary work, they are documenting their learning journeys. They need to be curious to make a documentary. In this case, they direct that curiosity inward to explore the impact of their experiences on their thinking, feelings, and growth, asking questions like:

- What am I learning? Why am I learning this? How is this relevant to my life?
- What am I understanding? What is confusing? What resources do I have access to if I need support?

9 George Couros, "What Does Your Digital Portfolio Show?" blog, georgecouros.ca/blog/archives/7450.

- How am I learning? Which strategies or resources are working best for me?
- In what areas am I demonstrating significant growth? In what areas am I struggling to make progress?
- What "aha's" or realizations am I having? How are those moments impacting my thinking?

As students compile documentation of their work over time in a digital portfolio, you can ask them to spend time engaging in self-assessment and reflection to appreciate the development of their content knowledge and skill set. You can ask them to compare different pieces in their portfolios that were created at different moments in the year to reflect on the differences between them. Here are some sample questions we've used to spark this reflection:

- What do you notice about the changes in your work?
- How have your skills changed and developed?
- Where is your growth as a learner most evident? What do you think contributed most to your growth this year?
- What does comparing these two pieces of work reveal about you as a learner?

The obvious goal of a portfolio is to document and share learning, but it also provides a wonderful resource for facilitating self-assessment and reflection. When students have opportunities to reflect on their learning growth and showcase the work they are most proud of in digital portfolios, they strengthen their self-assessment muscles and are actively involved in their own improvement process, which is critical for growth mindset and expert learning.

WRAP-UP

Traditional models of assessment put the teacher primarily in charge of articulating the criteria for success and evaluating the quality of student learning and growth. This model of dependence isn't sustainable for educators, and it prevents students from taking responsibility for self-awareness, self-reflection, and monitoring their progress, all of which they are capable of building with practice and support. If we want students to become more expert in their learning, we have to consistently shift the responsibility for reflection and assessment to them. Using the strategies in this chapter can help educators share the cognitive load of reflecting on and learning from assessments to the learners they serve.

REFLECT AND DISCUSS

1. Consider your current assessment practices. How often do you ask students to assess their own work? How does your approach to self-assessment compare to the strategies outlined in this chapter?
2. How could a consistent routine of student self-assessment, using the strategies outlined in this chapter, help to support student self-regulation and coping with frustration and challenge?
3. How do strong examples, vocabulary, and access to clear success criteria support successful student self-assessment?
4. How can you ask students to consistently assess their skills, content knowledge, and ability to self-regulate in your learning environment?

PUTTING IT INTO PRACTICE

Right now, you're likely spending a lot of time on assessment. We challenge you to begin to shift from teacher assessment to student self-assessment. Choose one of the strategies in this chapter and give it a try!

- Strategy #1: Exemplars, vocabulary, and success criteria
- Strategy #2: Reflective journaling, podcasting, or blogging
- Strategy #3: Ongoing self-assessment routine
- Strategy #4: Showcasing growth with student portfolios

Planning Template 8: Self-Assessment

What skills do you want students to develop as they engage in regular self-assessment?	
What strategy will you use to encourage students to assess their work? • Analyzing exemplars, building academic vocabulary, and defining success criteria • Reflecting in an ongoing journal, podcast, or blog • Updating an ongoing self-assessment document • Showcasing growth with student portfolios	
Which blended learning model or strategy will you use to create time for self-assessment in class? • Station rotation model • Choice boards • Playlist model • Whole-group rotation model	
How will you encourage students to reflect on what they learned about themselves from the process of assessing their own work? • What did they notice about their strengths? • What areas would benefit from further development? • What support or instruction do they need to continue improving?	

WORKFLOW SHIFT #9

From Teachers Initiating Parent Communication to Learners Owning the Conversation about Their Progress

Spitting Mad

Catlin

"Hello, Mrs. Tucker. Your son is in my office because he spit on another student."

What?

I was speechless. The principal was calm and patient as she explained that my son had an altercation with another kindergartener and spit on that child. My heart was racing as she explained in broad brushstrokes what had happened. I felt like *I* was in the principal's office. I had, apparently, raised a child who spits on people. The principal explained that she had spoken with my son and sent him back to class. She encouraged me to talk with him when I picked him up from school. *Oh, you better believe I am going to talk to him!*

My brain was buzzing. I could not concentrate. The rest of my workday was shot! *What on earth would make my child spit on another child?* My daughter, two years older than my son, had never been in the principal's office. Yes, there was a tiny biting incident in daycare, but other than that, I had never received any parent communication about her behavior. So, I was totally unprepared for this moment.

When I picked up my children at the end of the school day, I told my son that the principal had called me. He burst into tears. In an instant, all of my frustration and disappointment disappeared. I scooped him into my arms and asked him to tell me what had happened. He explained between gasps that his backpack hangs right above another student's backpack in the cubby where all the bags are stored. When they were getting their snacks for morning break, the other student had grabbed a piece of artwork out of my son's backpack and would not give it back. The student tore a picture that my son had worked hard on and planned to give me for my birthday the following week. My heart broke for him. After he got the story out, we talked about different ways he could have expressed his frustration and handled the situation.

Later that evening, after my kids were in bed, I was still thinking about this incident. It struck me that so much happened during my children's school days that I didn't know anything about. I did not know about their little successes or the challenging aspects of their day. I always asked my kids how their days were in the car on the way home or at the dinner table, but their answers—"Okay," "Normal," "Fine"—rarely contained much detail.

When I would ask more probing questions, like "What did you learn today?" or "What was your favorite part of your day?" I might get slightly more substantive answers, but not always. I longed to know more about their days at school. I wanted to support them academically, behaviorally, and socially, but that was challenging to do when I didn't really know what was happening beyond the code red "your kid was spitting on people" phone call from the principal. I wished for more windows into their days at school.

As a teacher, I knew how hard it was to keep parents informed about their student's growth and development beyond the progress reports or the occasional email at the end of each grading period. Parent communication was reserved for moments of crisis to discuss interventions to improve academic performance or behavior. Still, parents are more likely to be supportive partners in this work if we also find ways to share the positive moments as well. Yet consistently communicating with between 30 and 160 (or more) families is a time-consuming affair.

So, how do we shift students to the center of this experience and arm them with the tools they need to provide their parents with meaningful updates?

The Research and Reality: It Takes a Village

Parent involvement in children's education positively impacts academic performance, with students enrolling in higher-level programs, graduating from high school, and pursuing postsecondary education at higher rates.[1] In fact "home-based, rather than school-based, involvement in supporting learning has the greatest impact on student learning," and parents are more likely to be actively involved in their child's learning at home if teachers cultivate an instructional partnership with parents.[2] There is that word again! "Partnership." Not only do the most effective teachers form a partnership with the students they work with in order to share the responsibility for learning, but they also work to build a partnership with parents and guardians sharing the responsibility for supporting student progress.

The adults at home supporting the child are an essential part of the educational puzzle, yet they are not always included in the conversations about the students' learning goals or their progress toward those goals. Instead of relegating parent involvement to a couple events each year, like Back to School Night, we can take a

1 Christine Olmstead, "Using Technology to Increase Parent Involvement in Schools," *TechTrends* 57, no. 6 (October 18, 2013): 28–37.

2 Ibid, 29.

cue from the language in the Individuals with Disabilities Education Improvement Act (IDEA), which states that school systems must include parents in the individualized education program (IEP) team for a child with a disability. In fact, parent involvement and shared decision-making on the IEP team are two of the guiding principles of IDEA. However, just as the teacher-to-student ratio creates imbalances and time-consuming workflows, the sheer number of parents and guardians creates challenges in effective and consistent parent communication.

The good news is that research has shown that not only can school and teacher communication lead to higher levels of parent involvement, but so does student-initiated communication.[3] We know that schools and teachers will attempt to keep families in the loop when it comes to events and grades; however, it still isn't common practice to have students regularly communicating with parents. This is a missed opportunity. In fact, if students are going to be active agents in universally designed blended learning environments, they must take their metacognitive work and use what they are learning about themselves as students to update their parents about their progress. We believe that supporting students in owning the conversation about their own progress is an important part of cultivating expert learners.

So, how do we help students regularly communicate with their parents about their goals, progress, areas of strength, and areas in need of further improvement? What lines of communication are most effective for our students and their families? How do we articulate the value of having students lead this conversation?

---

3 Kelli E. Staples and Jennifer A. Diliberto, "Guidelines for Successful Parent Involvement: Working with Parents of Students with Disabilities," *Teaching Exceptional Children* 42, no. 6.

Strategy #1: Semi-monthly Audio or Email Updates

Students are rarely asked to take ownership of and responsibility for their work, behavior, or academic progress. A parent may not realize there is a problem until a zero lands in the grade book, report cards are sent home, or the principal calls because your kid spit on someone! Requiring students to regularly communicate with their parents about their progress in a class creates an incentive for them to prioritize their schoolwork and hone their self-regulation skills. This strategy also relieves the pressure from the teacher, who has myriad other tasks vying for their time and attention. And, if the only time a parent receives communication is when something negative has happened, it creates tension in the parent-teacher relationship. Instead, parent communication should provide a more complete picture of the student's performance at school.

If we are hoping to cultivate expert learners who are comfortable stretching their metacognitive muscles, they should be capable of owning the conversation about their progress.

Semi-monthly updates are regular enough to effectively keep parents in the loop while also feeling sustainable. It is important that the practice of updating parents about student progress be built into class time. Depending on the age of the students, these parent updates can take the form of an email or an audio recording. If you ask older students to craft a well-written email or leave a cogent audio message using a simple script, like the ones in Table 10, you can make this a task every other week at the online station in a station

If we are hoping to cultivate expert learners who are comfortable stretching their metacognitive muscles, they should be capable of owning the conversation about their progress.

rotation. Alternatively, you can use your teacher-led station or pull students individually from a playlist to facilitate audio updates. This makes using this strategy with younger learners or learners who need additional support more manageable. Once students have had support using this strategy, you can gradually release responsibility for this routine to the students.

As with all of the strategies we have highlighted, we suggest giving students agency with this routine. You can allow them to select a script that is appropriate for them. Some students might be excited to celebrate a success or share an area of growth, while others may be falling behind on an assignment or project and need more support. You can encourage students to select the type of script that will be most meaningful to them. You may also want to encourage groups of students to work collaboratively to write additional scripts for parent communication. It's helpful to provide a few examples to get them started as we did in Table 10, but positioning the students to contribute to a growing collection of parent-communication scripts will give them more ownership over the process and provide them with more options.

What's most rewarding about this strategy are the conversations between parents and their children. If you ask your students to email their parents, we suggest you require that your students cc you on the initial email. Parents often "reply all" and keep you in the loop as they dialogue with their children. We've noticed that parents ask thoughtful questions in their follow-up emails, like, "Why weren't you able to complete this part of the assignment when it was due? How are you using your class time? What can I do at home to support you in getting your work done?" There is so much value in encouraging students to have these conversations with their parents so they feel like they are integral members of the learning team. Our experience using this strategy is that parents have often thanked us for keeping them in the loop about their child's progress or lack thereof.

Table 10: Email and Audio Scripts

Email and Audio Update Scripts
Purpose: Celebrating Strengths and Areas of Growth **Script:** Hello [name of the person receiving the email or audio update], In [name of class], I've been working on [describe areas of focus]. I've demonstrated significant growth in [state a specific skill or area]. I believe [insert tasks, activities, behaviors that led to your growth] helped me to improve in this area. I plan to continue [state next steps for development or new area of focus]. If you have any questions or comments, please [insert directions for how parents can reply]. Love, [your name]
Purpose: High/Low Update **Script:** Hello [name of the person receiving the email or audio update], In the last two weeks, my high has been [insert a description of an assignment, task, behavior, interaction, routine, or self-management skill that reflects significant improvement or development]. This high makes me feel [insert an explanation of the impact]. A low, or an area where I feel like I need to spend more time growing and developing, is [insert a description of an assignment, task, behavior, interaction, routine, or self-management skill that needs additional work, practice, or development]. To continue making progress in this area, I will need to [action plan for continued improvement and/or request support]. If you have any questions or comments, please [insert directions for how parents can reply]. Love, [your name]

Purpose: Behind on an Assignment and Need Support

Script: Hello [name of the person receiving the email or audio update],

In [name of class], we are working on [insert the name of the assignment]. I am supposed to be [target for the class]. Currently, I am [state progress]. My plan for catching up is [describe the action plan with completion dates]. It would be helpful if you [insert the ways in which parents or guardians can support you at home].

If you have any questions or comments, please [insert directions for how parents can reply].

Love,

[your name]

Strategy #2: Grow-and-Glow Digital Slide Deck

Similar to a high/low update, a grow-and-glow structure encourages students to share an area in need of growth and an area of pride or a specific success. This strategy is often used to help students give each other meaningful feedback, but it works beautifully to format communication from students to their parents or guardians. It encourages students to provide a more balanced update, requiring that they reflect on what is going well and where they need to invest more time and energy to improve.

Using a grow-and-glow digital slide deck, like the one pictured in Figure 39, may make this routine more accessible and inclusive. Students can use the functionality of a digital slide deck to type, use voice-to-text, insert images of offline work or links to online work, or record a short video describing their areas of growth as well as their successes.

Figure 39: Glow-and-Grow Slide Deck

I'm glowing!

The thing I'm most proud of is _______.

I worked hard on _______ this week.

I _______ well this week.

I've gotten better at _______.

You can embed sentence frames to support students in articulating their areas of success and the areas that require further growth. The same digital slide deck can be used for student-parent communication over a trimester, semester, or even school year if students add the most recent glow-and-grow slides to the top of the deck with a date. Then you can share a single deck with each family at the beginning of the school year and let them know that their student will be updating the deck every other week to share their update with parents. Using a single slide deck minimizes complexity in sharing multiple slide decks with parent emails, but it also creates an ongoing portfolio of the student's progress in the class. We suggest giving parents the ability to add comments to the slide deck so they can compliment work samples, ask questions, and offer support.

Strategy #3: Student-Created Toolkit

In their paper titled "Guidelines for Successful Parent Involvement: Working with Parents of Students with Disabilities," Kelli Staples and Jennifer Diliberto share a strategy called Toolkits to help parents stay involved in their child's education. They encourage teachers to create a monthly toolkit to include strategies, tips, and activities parents can do with their children at home. The toolkit should reflect topics and themes addressed in the classroom during that month. Teachers distribute the toolkits at the beginning of each month, and include clear, precise, and explicit instructions for how to use the toolkits, which might include tips on homework routines, healthy living, embedding structure in the home environment, behavior management, academic games, and how to read aloud with your children.[4]

We love the idea of a monthly toolkit, but as with everything in this book, we want to encourage you to find a way to position the learners to do the work. Have students compile a personalized toolkit that is specific to their needs. What strategies, tips, or activities would be most meaningful for them? What would they like to focus on at home that they believe will help them be more successful academically, socially, and behaviorally? As with all routines and procedures in a classroom, you'll need to onboard students to the practice of creating their toolkits. It may be useful to modify the template pictured in Figure 40 to help students think through the parts of their toolkits and to explain their areas of focus, include resources and activities that target those areas, and make suggestions for how family members can use the toolkit to support them at home.

If you are working with younger students or students who need more support, you may want to focus on co-creating these toolkits as part of your conferencing sessions with students. You could assign a choice board or a playlist for students to self-pace through to create the time and space needed to have these important conversations.

4 Ibid., 61.

Figure 40: Student-Designed Toolkit

My Toolkit for [Month]		
Toolkit items	**Insert your personalized focus + resources and suggested activities**	**How can your family use this item to support you?**
Overarching topics, themes, and/or texts this month		
Content-specific strategy or skill focus		
Vocabulary development: Focus words		
Behavior management or self-regulation skill focus		
Self-care focus		
Personal goal for this month		
Academic goal for this month		
Behavioral or self-regulation goal for this month		

Strategy #4: Student-Designed Digital Newsletter

We remember receiving monthly newsletters from our kids' teachers throughout the school year. In the early grades, they were pinned to our kid's clothing. As our children got older, these newsletters wound up crumpled at the bottom of backpacks.

These newsletters often included important events and due dates, insights into the content and skills our children were focused on that month, images of the students at work in the classroom, and requests for parent volunteers. Although we both enjoyed getting updates from our kids' teachers, the newsletters were generic and not specific to our children, which meant we dutifully skimmed them but didn't necessarily look forward to receiving them.

Given the myriad digital tools available to students, they can quickly design their own multimedia digital newsletters or collaborate with a small group of peers to create a more personalized newsletter to share with families. You may want to provide an exemplar, a list of items to include, or a template for them to copy and use, like the one in Figure 41.

A multimedia newsletter can combine a range of strategies from goal-setting to reflection to sharing documentation of their in-class learning. You can give students agency over this process by providing a list of suggested items to include or a template to start with, but encourage them to customize their newsletter to focus on items that feel meaningful to *them*. You may also give them agency over the process by allowing them to decide whether they want to work independently, with a partner, or as part of a small group. In addition, you can provide a collection of digital tools to choose from and allow them to decide which technology tool they want to use to create and share their newsletters.

Figure 41: Digital Newsletter Template

Newsletter for [Month]

[Insert an inspiration quote or favorite saying]

Important dates:

My favorite assignment was...

My learning goals for this month:

My most challenging assignment was...

The thing I'm most proud of is...

The thing I need to work on most is...

[Insert media or links to digital work]

[Insert image]

[Insert image]

Strategy #5: Student-Family Digital Journal

Communication with families may be more challenging if the teacher speaks one language and families speak another. This is another area where it can be incredibly helpful to position the student to take the lead communicating with the people at home. The student can write or speak in the language appropriate for the individuals receiving updates about their progress. One strategy for encouraging a two-way line of communication is a digital journal between student and caregiver, as pictured in Figure 42.

Figure 42: Student-Family Journal

Student-Family Journal		
Date	**Student Entry**	**Family Response**

Once a week or twice a month, you can ask students to update a digital journal with a brief explanation of their performance. It will be helpful if you include prompts or questions for them to consider as they journal, including:

- What is going well in class?
- What concepts or skills have you learned in the last week or two?
- What activities or learning experiences have been particularly helpful in supporting learning?
- What has been most challenging in the last week or two?
- What resources or support have you used to navigate these challenges?
- Where do you plan to invest time and energy developing in the areas that need more growth?
- What support might your family provide you to ensure you keep making progress?

The benefit of having a two-way online journal is that you can view the interactions back and forth and add comments or address questions as needed. Additionally, if students add to the same shared digital journal all year, it documents their learning journey over time. This can be a useful resource to reference while conferencing with students or encouraging metacognitive skill building, since students can review their entries to appreciate how they have grown and developed over the course of the school year.

WRAP UP

Parents and families are a critical part of our students' educational journeys. They can support the learner in the home environment if they have the information and the tools to do so effectively. Parents benefit from regular communication about their students, but that workflow is hard to maintain for a teacher working with dozens of families. Instead, we want to arm students with the skills and routines necessary to own these conversations and keep their families informed about their progress. Communicating with families can build a routine of reflecting on learning, sharing documentation of learning, and articulating progress clearly and cogently. These are important skills for our expert learners to practice and hone.

REFLECT AND DISCUSS

1. How often do you currently communicate with families? What form does this communication typically take?
2. What is often the catalyst for communication with families?
3. What have been the biggest barriers to regular communication with families? How might the strategies suggested in this chapter help you to mitigate or eliminate those barriers?
4. How might regular student communication about progress impact your students' feelings about the work they are doing? How might it impact how families feel about their students' experience at school?
5. How can you build student communication with families into the fabric of your class? How can you use blended learning models to create the time and space for students to engage in this work?

PUTTING IT INTO PRACTICE

Choose one of the strategies outlined in this chapter to move toward more student-led communication with families.

- Strategy #1: Semi-monthly audio or email updates
- Strategy #2: Grow-and-glow digital slide deck
- Strategy #3: Student-created toolkit
- Strategy #4: Student-designed digital newsletter
- Strategy #5: Student-family digital journal

Planning Template 9: Parent Communication

What skills do you want students to develop as they own the conversation about their progress with their parents, families, or caregivers?	
What strategy will you use to encourage students to provide parents, families, or caregivers with regular updates about their progress? • Semi-monthly audio or email updates • Grow-and-glow digital slide deck • Student-created toolkit • Student-designed digital newsletter • Student-family digital journal	
Which blended learning model or strategy will you use to create time for students to communicate their progress with their parents, families, or caregivers? • Station rotation model • Choice boards • Playlist model • Whole-group rotation model	
What supports, scripts, or scaffolds will your students need to successfully communicate with their parents, families, or caregivers?	

WORKFLOW SHIFT #10

From Teacher Project Design to Student-Led Project-Based Learning

Toot Toot Tootsie

Katie

In college, I briefly dated a ninety-five-year-old man. That got your attention, didn't it? The relationship was fleeting—a single night. It was the evening that my classmates and I hosted a Roaring Twenties party at a local nursing home, and my actual boyfriend was at the party. So, I guess it was doomed from the start.

I went to the University of New Hampshire for my undergraduate degree and studied recreational therapy. A rec therapist uses activities to support well-being, health, and balance in individuals with physical, behavioral, social, and/or emotional support needs. In one class, we put our knowledge of rec therapy into practice.

Our professor gave us a single goal: Take what we had learned and make a difference. We had to choose the client, the venue, and the activity. At first, I think we all probably looked around like Rudolph in the headlights. I mean, we got to decide everything? Where was the list of potential clients? Where was the list of ideas? Our budget?

We were twenty years old, for goodness' sake! Our brains weren't even fully developed!

My classmates and I settled on a local nursing home, took the Wildcat Transit bus to meet with the staff, and started planning. We decided to throw a Roaring Twenties party to bring back happy memories of the residents' youth. Over months, we wrangled a DJ and learned the song catalog to the Billboard Top 40 of 1925 (clearly, no such thing existed, but we made our own). We bargain shopped for feather boas, created slideshows of the good ole days, and created little invitations that looked like tuxedos. We met with some of the residents and the cooking staff to create a five-course meal, and we decorated the heck out of the recreation hall.

Before we knew it, the night arrived. As the DJ played a slow song, a man in a walker slid over to me—clearly quite the heart-breaker in his day—and asked me to dance. Of course, I couldn't turn him down. He turned to my boyfriend and said, "She's mine now."

My college boyfriend answered, "I mean, how can I compete?" He couldn't.

I still have the pictures of that night, my classmates and I, our arms wrapped around each other surrounding a microphone, singing "Toot, Toot, Tootsie!" and "Cheek to Cheek."

The evening was so damn special. Not because we received an A on our project, not because I had not one but two loving men in my life that night, but because we made memories, and we made them happen in an authentic, magical way. Our professor could have assigned a project, given us parameters, and clipped our wings, but she hadn't.

It was the power of student-led project-based learning.

The Research and Reality: The Nonexistent Average

The goal of project-based learning (PBL) is to engage students in investigating authentic problems with solutions that have the potential to be implemented and used in real life.[1] As with other traditional workflows, teachers sometimes assume responsibility for much of the design in project-based learning. We were both guilty of this before we learned more about PBL, UDL, and blended learning and freed ourselves from having to come up with the perfect project. Research is clear that PBL is most successful when educators have confidence in accepting a role as a collaborator in the learning process rather than as a figure of authority or knowledge.[2] We need to embed more flexibility in the design of learning and authentic projects. This optimizes both equity and inclusion and demonstrates a belief that all students are capable of asking questions, defining problems, and collaborating to develop solutions.

We need to embed more flexibility in the design of learning and authentic projects. This optimizes both equity and inclusion and demonstrates a belief that all students are capable of asking questions, defining problems, and collaborating to develop solutions.

Michelle Bartlett, PhD, a faculty scholar at North Carolina State University, shared the importance of co-creating PBL units with learners. She noted, "Let's not miss out on the brilliant solutions to complex issues that will come from minds that wouldn't be reached by an education designed for the

1 Bassam Hussein, "Addressing Collaboration Challenges in Project-Based Learning: The Student's Perspective," *Education Sciences* 11, article 434.

2 John Mitchell and Lynne Rogers, "Staff Perceptions of Implementing Project-Based Learning in Engineering Education," *European Journal of English Education* 45, 349–62.

elusive, non-existent average."[3] When we facilitate PBL through the lens of UDL and blended learning, we ensure all students have opportunities to lose themselves in authentic, meaningful learning experiences. PBL moves beyond a project as an assessment to include a focus on the project as the vehicle for learning.

The Buck Institute of Education, a leader in PBL, differentiates between what they call "dessert projects" and "main course projects," which create the foundation for PBL.

> We find it helpful to distinguish a "dessert project"—a short, intellectually-light project served up after the teacher covers the content of a unit in the usual way—from a "main course" project, in which the project is the unit. In Project Based Learning, the project is the vehicle for teaching the important knowledge and skills students need to learn. The project contains and frames curriculum and instruction.[4]

This is not to say that you cannot assign a "dessert project," but the focus of this chapter is on designing and facilitating PBL, leveraging UDL and blended learning so that students learn from and share their learning within a project-based unit that they help to design.

Although there are numerous definitions and components of PBL, we will use the seven essential design elements of "gold-standard" PBL units identified by the Buck Institute. Table 11 crosswalks these elements to UDL and blended learning. Connecting the three design frameworks reminds us that students need to drive the development of PBL units.

As you can see, there is an opportunity to leverage PBL and deeper learning through UDL and blended learning. We offer four

3 Michelle Bartlett, "Perspective," EducationNC, July 20, 2020, ednc.org/universal-design-for-learning-project-based-learning/.

4 Buck Institute for Education, "What Is PBL?," PBLWorks, accessed March 7, 2022, pblworks.org/what-is-pbl.

strategies to shift your workflow from teacher-designed "dessert projects" to student-driven "main course projects" with PBL.

Student direction is inherent in PBL, but as with other workflows, teachers often design these units for the mythical "average" learner. When we implement the following strategies, we shift more ownership to students so they can personalize the experience by pursuing projects of interest to them.

Table 11: PBL, UDL, and BL

PBL Core Component	UDL Connection	BL Connection
Challenging problem or question	When we can design learning so students can solve problems that are personally meaningful, we optimize motivation and expert learning.	Allowing students to identify a problem or question of interest they want to pursue gives them control over the path of their learning.
Sustained inquiry	Engagement requires learners to sustain effort and persistence as they commit to ongoing learning.	Inquiry benefits from variable time on task. Giving students more control over the time and pace of online and offline exploration leads to a deeper understanding of the problem or question.

Authenticity	Engagement guidelines prompt educators to co-create relevant, authentic, and meaningful options for learners.	Giving students the agency to select their focus for PBL creates personal authenticity as students focus on issues, concerns, interests, or cultures relevant to their lives. In addition, blended learning requires a partnership between teacher and student, so teachers can work alongside learners to identify authentic context to ground their projects.
Student voice and choice	Choice and voice are cornerstones of UDL and expert learning.	Student agency, or their ability to make decisions, is an essential characteristic of student-centered blended learning. To be active agents in the learning process, they must enjoy choice and voice.
Reflection	Expert learners consistently monitor progress through self-assessment and self-reflection.	Reflection and metacognitive skill building are critical to the students' ability to self-regulate effectively, which is critical to their success in blended learning environments.

Critique and revision	Mastery-oriented feedback and a focus on strategic revision is critical to expert learning.	In addition to asking for feedback from other members of the learning community offline, students have access to an authentic audience online where they can request and receive feedback on their work-in-progress.
Public product	When we provide multiple means of engagement, students need options to share the outcomes of their learning with authentic audiences.	Digital tools and online platforms give students the opportunity to share their product with a global audience.

Strategy #1: Create a Project Buffet

As classroom teachers we assigned one-size-fits-all dessert projects where all students had to do things like write a poem, record a video, or write a letter to a state senator. Sometimes, we were a little more creative. Think puppet shows at a local elementary school and art exhibits at a local library. There is absolutely nothing wrong with these as outcomes. The problem is that we came up with all the ideas! And then of course, after sharing these brilliant ideas, we got the inevitable, "That is booooorrrriiinnnng."

Before diving into the world of PBL, put students to work brainstorming potential project outcomes. This is a fabulous idea for two reasons. First, it puts our sweet scholars to work in researching potential ways to express their knowledge. Even more fabulous, we can steal their amazing ideas when creating choice boards! With students, you can co-design a bulletin board, a "menu" of choices on Canva, or a shared Google Doc. When it comes time for students to decide how they want to share their learning in authentic ways, they will have a resource to get them started. We have created the template pictured in Table 12 to share with students. We encourage you to continue building it with your students' brilliant ideas. If you teach early elementary, you can complete this template with colleagues, parent volunteers, or your virtual professional learning network. Then, as you are working through your PBL unit, you can empower students to continually reflect on the driving questions, the "firm goals," their preferred audiences, and how they can create and refine a product that is relevant, authentic, and meaningful. That beats assigning every student a TED Talk or children's book!

Table 12: Project Product Ideas

Product Idea	Options
Writing	• Write a formal letter to an authentic audience. • Write a blog and share with an authentic audience. • Write a children's book to read to elementary students or donate to a local library. • Write a detailed proposal about how to solve an authentic problem. Submit to an online publication. • Write a poem or song in response to driving questions and perform in a local coffee shop or another venue.
Video	• Create a public service announcement for local access television or another authentic audience. • Record a TED Talk or submit to present at a TEDx conference. • Produce a short documentary and publish it on YouTube.

Audio	• Record a podcast with a community member where you discuss the driving question and share on social media. • Record an investigative report-style podcast on your challenge or question, integrating the parts of the PBL process to provide a clear picture for your audience, then publish and share on social media.

Strategy #2: Embrace a Flexible PBL Sentence Frame

Zachary Herrmann, the executive director of the Center for Professional Learning at the Penn Graduate School of Education, offers a helpful sentence frame to conceptualize project-based learning. In PBL, "Students explore [Question/Problem]. To do this, they will take on the role of [Role], make personal connections by [Personal Connections], and work to produce [Product] in service of [Audience and Impact]. In doing so, they will learn [Project Learning Goals]."[5] We love the use of sentence frames to scaffold the way students conceptualize PBL, but it has the potential to lead us down a slippery slope of one-size-fits-all thinking. For example, let's take the sentence frame offered by Herrmann and demonstrate a nonexample of a student-directed PBL unit and how it differs from an example using UDL and BL.

5 Zachary Herrmann, "6 Ways to Guide Students to More Authentic Work in PBL," edutopia.org/article/6-ways-guide-students-more-authentic-work-pbl, October 27, 2021.

Table 13: Flexible Sentence Frames

Nonexample of Student-Generated PBL
Students explore why it's important to wear a bike helmet. To do this, they will take on the role of producer of a public service announcement, make personal connections by thinking about how to connect with peers, and work to produce a thirty-second video PSA using iMovie to share on the cable access television station. In doing so, they will learn how to craft arguments to support claims in an analysis of substantive topics or texts, using valid reasoning and relevant and sufficient evidence.
Example of UDL, BL, PBL
Students explore the negative impacts of adolescent behaviors. To do this, they will take on the role of a marketing executive, make personal connections by thinking about how to change the behavior of their peers, and work to produce an authentic product. In doing so, they will learn how to craft arguments to support claims in an analysis of substantive topics or texts, using valid reasoning, as well as relevant and sufficient evidence.

In the nonexample, we fell back into our habits of making decisions for students about their learning and their product. Granted, the project is more engaging than a multiple-choice test, but it puts a lot of pressure on us as teachers to come up with an authentic idea, and we know that many students will not be invested in learning about bike helmets or making a PSA video. Exploring the impact of bike helmets would not be engaging for a student who does not own a bike, does not know how to ride a bike, or has no interest in ever learning to ride a bike. The project is incredibly well intentioned, but it lacks authenticity for all students and fails to offer voice and choice.

In PBL, students need ongoing opportunities to solve real-world problems while mastering standards and sharing their work with an authentic audience. To help students set goals for their authentic projects, you can pair a flexible PBL sentence frame with the PBL project menu. For example, you could ask students to complete an online or offline fill-in-the-blank activity using the template pictured in Figure 43. Once they've completed the Mad Libs-style brainstorming activity, ask them to post it to your LMS or a digital Post-it note wall so students can explore each other's ideas. This is an opportunity for students to identify peers who are interested in similar questions or problems and who might enjoy working together. It can also serve as inspiration for students who are unsure what they want to focus on for their projects.

Figure 43: Fill-in-the-Blanks Brainstorming Activity

Fill-in-the-Blanks
Students explore ____________________. [Question/Problem]
To do this, they will take on the role of __________, make personal connections by __________, and work to produce __________ in service of ____________________. [Audience and Impact]
In doing so, they will learn ____________________. [Project Learning Goals]
Credit for sentence frame: Zachary Herrmann

In our UDL/BL example, we use the same sentence frame but leave room for students to decide what they want to study, their role, and how they want to share their learning. In both scenarios, they are working toward the same firm goals, but when we design the frame with UDL and blended learning as drivers, students have incredible flexibility in their journey, ensuring the essential elements of PBL design.

You may be nervous to release control over the parts of the project to students. What if they don't select a question or problem that falls within the umbrella of the unit's topic or subject? What if they don't balance online research with offline exploration? What if they don't anchor their project in an authentic context? We know relinquishing control and trusting students to make decisions can be a little nerve-racking, but you can scaffold this process with a project proposal, like the one pictured in Figure 44.

A project proposal provides students with the opportunity to think through the essential PBL design elements and consider the form these will take in their projects. You also have the opportunity to review the proposals with students prior to beginning the project. When done side by side, this review of student proposals reinforces a partnership model, creating space for teacher and learner to discuss, adjust, and refine the proposal to ensure students have thought through the parts and have a solid plan.

Figure 44: Project Proposal

Project Proposal		
Essential PBL Design Elements	Questions to Consider	Your Proposed Plan
Challenging problem or question	What problem or question do you want to pursue and/or attempt to answer?	
Sustained inquiry	How will you attempt to learn about and understand this problem or question? What information would be helpful to collect?	
Authenticity	What is the context of your project? How is it grounded in the real world? What real-world processes, tasks, and/or tools will you use?	

Student voice and choice	What key decisions will you need to make as you move through this project?	
Reflection	How will you reflect on your learning as you move through this project? What reflection strategy would be most effective for you?	
Critique and revision	At what points during this project would feedback be most useful? Who would you like to gather feedback from during this project?	
Public product	How will you demonstrate what you learned? What product will you create?	

Strategy #3: Create an Authentic PBL Network

This strategy is adapted from a process called Future Search, which helps large groups accomplish tasks.[6] Often the process brings together sixty to one hundred people in one room, but you can always go virtual! The idea is that the group comes together to build consensus before collectively creating an action plan. The action plan, or outcome, would be potential projects and collaborations that inspire students to find purpose and take action.

We see this process as an incredible opportunity to create action plans for PBL units. The adapted Future Search process begins by identifying potential collaborators and sending out invitations to invite them to be PBL partners. If you have students in early elementary, you could complete this process with your teaching team and parent volunteers.

6 Future Search Network, "What Is Future Search?," Future Search, accessed March 7, 2022, futuresearch.net/about/whatis/.

Creating connections with stakeholders provides endless opportunities for students to work to solve real problems in their community. As an example, if you develop a relationship with a local coffee shop owner, they may share their desire to build a younger community of patrons who feel like the space was created with and for them. Knowing this, students in art and design courses can propose rotating artist galleries and open mic nights that showcase student work, create prototypes of potential seasonal and cultural window displays, and collaborate with the owner to facilitate listening sessions with students to determine their interests and needs.

You might start a short list of potential collaborators, but allow students or partners to contribute as well. These stakeholders could include:

- Local business owners
- Religious officials
- Parents
- Elected officials
- Media personalities (writers in local newspapers, cable access contacts, etc.)
- Community leaders (librarians, policemen, firemen, etc.)

Next, create small groups assigned to a single category. Group 1, for example, may be tasked with finding the contact information for local business owners. The group can decide how they research and divide and conquer the tasks. Once each group has created a list, the core planning team decides the best way to bring the group together. You may want to schedule an in-person or Zoom meeting where people can find out more about the process to create a vision for PBL in the classroom. Task students with choosing the date and designing an invitation for the brainstorming session.

Next, each group reaches out to individuals on the list to invite them to the meeting. The Future Search Network recommends personal touches—phone calls, handwritten notes, etc. Young students could record short videos, while older students can schedule Zoom meetings or phone calls to extend the invite. Essentially, your students create pathways for two-way communication with members of the community they can connect and collaborate with.

Once the RSVPs start rolling in, create small groups for the meeting. Each group should include students as well as individuals from other categories. You may have one group, for example, with four students, a school principal, a member of the town's financial committee, the owner of a local coffee shop, a police officer, and a parent.

Work with students to create a meeting agenda. The agenda items in Table 14 are adapted from the Future Search methodology. It is critical that students take on leadership roles in the planning and facilitation of the process and the meeting.

Table 14: PBL Future Search (Adapted from Future Search Network)

Agenda Item	Spice It Up with UDL + BL
Focus on the Past People make timelines of key events in their own lives. Small groups tell stories about each timeline and the implications of their stories for the work they have come to do.	This is an opportunity for self-reflection. It allows all members to consider their own identity and share the work they do and what is important to them. If you have younger students, they may share about their interests and what they want to do when they grow up.
Make Connections The whole group makes a "mind map" of connections between them. What is important to all group members?	This step fosters collaboration and community, helping to build authentic connections between students and community members.

Proud and Sorries Stakeholder groups report what they are proud of and sorry about in their own lives and work. What challenges do they face? What problems do they wish they could solve?	This brainstorming session helps to identify real-world problems that impact the community at large and continues to foster self-reflection and collaboration.
Future Scenarios Groups put themselves into the future and imagine that they have solved the challenges and problems they brainstormed. Each person describes the future as if it has already been accomplished.	This step can help students to imagine potential projects and how they can work together with the community to create a better future.
Action Planning The group begins to plan potential projects. They can work with community members to create authentic roles, personal connections, products, and audience.	As an educator, you define "firm goals," but students work with an authentic audience to create the scope of potential projects they can work on throughout the year. This also sparks meaningful two-way collaboration as students can build on these connections throughout the school year.

When we position learners to lead the process of reaching out to members of the community and draft an agenda for their time together, they are likely to feel more ownership over the process and more pride over the outcomes.

WRAP-UP

Too often in classrooms, we as teachers make decisions about how students learn and share their knowledge in "dessert projects," which culminate a unit of study but don't drive it. Project-based learning puts students in the driver's seat. They understand the purpose of knowing the content standards as they relate to real world problems that personally matter to them. Because of student variability, PBL units need to be flexible enough for students to make decisions about what they learn, how they learn, and how they share what they know. When we leverage UDL and BL, we can implement the design elements of PBL while creating flexible pathways for students to create meaningful learning experiences for themselves.

REFLECT AND DISCUSS

1. What is the difference between a "dessert project" and a "main course" project? How do you currently use projects? Do they drive learning and/or assessment?
2. How does working with students to create a project buffet help to drive motivation and interest for upcoming PBL units?
3. Consider the last project you designed and plug the elements into the sentence frame shared in strategy #1: "Students explore [Question/Problem]. To do this, they will take on the role of [Role], make personal connections by [Personal Connections], and work to produce [Product] in service of [Audience and Impact]. In doing so, they will learn [Project Learning Goals]." Discuss how much flexibility was provided to learners. If needed, revise with a UDL and blended learning twist!
4. How might you utilize blended learning models to create the time and space needed to sit with individual learners to review and discuss their project proposals?

5. How can you create a PBL network where students make connections with and brainstorm potential project ideas with community partners?

PUTTING IT INTO PRACTICE

The next time you design PBL, use these strategies to ensure that your learners do most of the design work. We assure you that engagement will increase, and you will find more balance when you shift from the expert to the facilitator and collaborator.

- Strategy #1: Create a project buffet
- Strategy #2: Embrace a flexible PBL sentence frame
- Strategy #3: Create an authentic PBL network

Planning Template 10: PBL

What is the problem or question?	
What role will students assume?	
What personal connections do students have to the problem or question?	
What will students produce?	
Who is the audience? What impact will the product have?	
What are the project learning goals? What will students know, understand, or be able to do?	

CONCLUSION

I'll Finish It

Katie

I currently live with a little NBA encyclopedia. My six-year-old son is a fact machine who walks around the house with the vibe of the little kid in *Jerry Maguire* who pelts Tom Cruise's character with facts such as, "Do you know dogs and bees can smell fear?" The facts that my son throws out all have one thing in common: basketball.

Did you know that Gheorghe Mureşan and Manute Bol were the tallest guys in the NBA at 7'7"?

Did you know that Larry Bird had 21,791 career points?

Did you know that Kevin Durant was College Player of the Year when he was a freshman at Texas?

Welp, buddy, I do now.

As I was writing this conclusion, my son was watching an NBA highlights video. One clip caught my eye. In 2016, Kevin Durant had a little trash-talk session with Jerami Grant during a game. A reporter asked him about it during the postgame conference. His response was good-natured. He said that as long as things stayed within the lines of the court, it was all good. He went on to make a joke about how he didn't initiate the exchange of words, but he quipped, "If you start it, I'll finish it." I adore this sentiment! Cat, I see your introduction to this book. I'll finish it.

As Cat shared in the introduction, teachers are working too hard to not have better academic results, higher levels of student engagement, and more balance in their lives. *Education Week* published a special report with an article called "Teachers' Mental Health Has Suffered in the Pandemic: Here's How Districts Can Help" that begins, "Teachers' stress and anxiety have soared and their morale has plummeted during the pandemic, a flammable combination that could burn them out and lead them to leave their jobs."[1]

The article goes on to recommend mindfulness, yoga, exercise, and healthy eating as well as the importance of addressing mental health head-on and offering frequent check-ins. These are all important drivers of balance and address mental health, but they do not address another elephant in the room: teachers are overburdened. For some of you, adding on a yoga session would only be one more thing you have to do. I can see it now. "Are you serious, Administrator? I don't have time for flippin' yoga!"

We want to shift the narrative. We want you to have the time and energy to attend yoga sessions if you wish, take a nice walk, or enjoy a Diet Pepsi or a margarita with your besties over an episode of *Schitt's Creek*. We want you to have the time to prioritize your mental health, which is difficult to do when you feel like you don't have the space to take a deep breath.

We wrote this book to help you learn how to take things off your plate, specifically the control and responsibility for all teaching and learning in your class. Workflows are putting too much stress on educators: Teachers currently carry the weight of transferring

1 Catherine Gewertz, "Teachers' Mental Health Has Suffered in the Pandemic: Here's How Districts Can Help," *EdWeek*, May 4, 2021, edweek.org/leadership/teachers-mental-health-has-suffered-in-the-pandemic-heres-how-districts-can-help/2021/05.

information, leading whole-group instruction, providing feedback and grading student work, and communicating with parents. And this is often done in a one-size-fits-all way because that's how many of us learned to do it. Here's the thing. You don't have to do it that way anymore. You can and you should transfer this responsibility to the students you serve. And if you're feeling guilty about that—don't.

All the work we are doing for our students is *not* preparing them for the world of work or the lives they want to live. We are the ones who are taking initiative, building relationships, and monitoring progress. When we use these more traditional practices, students may perform well on standardized assessments or earn solid GPAs, but that is not enough. Good students are not necessarily expert learners, and it's showing. Let's take a look at the research and the stark reality of readiness for college, careers, and life.

Oftentimes, the success of public education is measured by outcomes of standardized tests and college placement, yet even when students pass these measures, the outcomes are sobering. Many school districts tout their acceptance rates to four-year colleges as a gold standard of PK–12 success. Yet, according to the National Center for Educational Statistics, of the students who enter college in a bachelor's degree program at a four-year institution, only 63 percent complete that degree.[2] That's not even two-thirds.

Those who do graduate face their own barriers. In a national survey of C-level business executives, only 11 percent of respondents believed that college graduates have the skills they need to succeed.[3] The outcomes do not question graduate knowledge or technical skills. Rather, the reason that graduates fail is because of softer skills, specifically motivation, initiative, and coachability. I know this is

2 National Center for Education Statistics, "Undergraduate Retention and Graduation Rates," May 2021, nces.ed.gov/programs/coe/indicator/ctr.

3 Brandon Busteed, "University Academic Leaders Are Losing Confidence in Student Work Readiness—And That's Good News," *Forbes*, January 23, 2020, forbes.com/sites/brandonbusteed/2020/01/23/university-academic-leaders-are-losing-confidence-in-student-work-readiness--and-thats-good-news.

coming off a little Debbie Downer, but read on. The research is clear that college graduates need to be more self-directed, show more initiative, and need to be open to continuous, or expert, learning. We can argue the same for all students at all ages, as, clearly, these skills are not built overnight. These competencies, however, are consistently built in universally designed blended learning environments.

Whether you are a PK teacher or you're preparing students for higher education or the world of work, you have an incredible opportunity to design a classroom that helps them build the skills they need to be successful long after they leave your class. And in this scenario, YOU get to take some of your life, your sanity, and your happiness back.

The stakes are high for us and our students. Educators cannot continue to carry the cognitive load and workload of learning.

The stakes are high for us and our students. Educators cannot continue to carry the cognitive load and workload of learning. It affects educators' mental health, resilience, sense of balance, and joy. It is also preventing students from building their expert learning muscles, social-emotional competency, and deep engagement in learning.

UDL is a framework that provides a blueprint for educators to design teaching and learning opportunities so students can personalize their learning. At its core, UDL is about providing options and choices to students so they can set meaningful goals for how they will meet the standards, determine the methods and materials they need to reach their goals, and express how they met those goals in authentic ways. To do these things, students must become expert learners.

Growth mindset, or the belief that success is far more about effort than innate talent, is the brainchild of Carol Dweck, a professor of psychology at Stanford University. This concept—that success is something that can be achieved with persistence and motivation—is the foundation of UDL and blended learning. Dweck classifies all goals and activities into two categories: things we can do already and things we can't do *yet*. The theory is that anything is achievable with the right mindset and the right strategy. Dedication to committing to a task, learning from mistakes, and sticking with goals despite barriers is key to turning *not yet* into *already*.

We are confident that the workflow shifts in this book will create a more sustainable work environment for teachers and will increase the outcomes for all students. You may not have a student-driven classroom *yet*, but know that it is possible. You can use the strategies in this book to support students in taking more ownership of their learning and success. And in making these shifts, you not only share the burden and find balance, but you create a classroom that helps your students to build the skills and competencies they need to be successful in our world.

Please take this book to heart, put it into practice, and shift your workflows. At first, you may need to scaffold the transitions to facilitate change, but we have provided you with the tools to do that. As Cat shared in the introduction, "We also need to remember that these shifts will be new for our students and cause them to stretch. This may feel uncomfortable at first, because you are asking students to assume more cognitive and social responsibility for their learning. They will need clear routines, support, and skill-building to feel confident leading the learning in these reimagined workflows." The balance may not shift completely overnight, but over time, it will. We promise. Have faith that if you start the learning process, your brilliant students will finish it.

BIBLIOGRAPHY

Agarwal, Pooja K., and Patrice Bain. *Powerful Teaching: Unleash the Science of Learning*. Indianapolis, IN: John Wiley & Sons, 2019.

Alcala, Leah. "Highlighting Mistakes: A Grading Strategy." Video, 7:00. The Teaching Channel, 2015. learn.teachingchannel.com/video/math-test-grading-tips.

Babad, Elisha Y., Jacinto Inbar, and Robert Rosenthal. "Pygmalion, Galatea, and the Golem: Investigations of Biased and Unbiased Teachers." *Journal of Educational Psychology* 74, no. 4 (August 1982): 459–74.

Bartlett, Michelle. "Perspective." EducationNC. July 20, 2020. ednc.org/universal-design-for-learning-project-based-learning/.

Berger, Ron. "Deeper Learning: Highlighting Student Work." George Lucas Educational Foundation. January 3, 2013. edutopia.org/blog/deeper-learning-student-work-ron-berger.

Bishop, Rudine Sims. "Windows, Mirrors, and Sliding Glass Doors." *Perspectives: Choosing and Using Books in the Classroom* 6, no. 3 (1990).

Black, Paul, and Dylan Wiliam, "Inside the Black Box: Raising Standards through Classroom Assessment." *Phi Delta Kappan* 80, no. 2: 144, 146–148.

Buck Institute for Education. "What Is PBL?." PBLWorks. Accessed March 7, 2022. pblworks.org/what-is-pbl.

Busteed, Brandon. "University Academic Leaders Are Losing Confidence in Student Work Readiness—And That's Good News." *Forbes*. January 23, 2020. forbes.com/sites/brandonbusteed/2020/01/23/university-academic-leaders-are-losing-confidence-in-student-work-readiness--and-thats-good-news.

Carpenter, Tara S., Lisa Carter Beall, and Linda C. Hodges. "Using a Learning Management System for Exam Wrapper Feedback to Prompt Metacognitive Awareness in Large Courses." *Journal of Teaching and Learning with Technology* 9 (special issue): 79–91.

CASEL. "The CASEL Guide to Schoolwide Social and Emotional Learning." Accessed March 3, 2022. schoolguide.casel.org/.

Chand Dayal, Hem. "How Teachers Use Formative Assessment Strategies during Teaching: Evidence from the Classroom." *Australian Journal of Teacher Education* 46, no. 7: 1–21.

Chatzipanteli, Athanasia, Vasilis Grammatikopoulos, and Athanasios Gregoriadis, "Development and Evaluation of Metacognition in Early Childhood Education." *Early Child Development and Care* 184, no. 8: 1223–32.

Couros, George. "What Does Your Digital Portfolio Show?" Blog. georgecouros.ca/blog/archives/7450.

Donovan, Jeremy. *How to Deliver a TED Talk: Secrets of the World's Most Inspiring Presentations*. New York: McGraw Hill, 2014.

Dyer, Kathy. "What You Need to Know When Establishing Success Criteria in the Classroom." Teach. Learn. Grow. NWEA. August 4, 2020. nwea.org/blog/2018/what-you-need-to-know-when-establishing-success-criteria-in-the-classroom/.

Ferriter, William M. *The Big Book of Tools for Collaborative Teams in a PLC at Work*. Bloomington, IN: Solution Tree Press, 2020.

Future Search Network. "What Is Future Search?" Future Search. Accessed March 7, 2022. futuresearch.net/about/whatis/.

Gewertz, Catherine. "Teachers' Mental Health Has Suffered in the Pandemic: Here's How Districts Can Help." *EdWeek*. May 4, 2021. edweek.org/leadership/teachers-mental-health-has-suffered-in-the-pandemic-heres-how-districts-can-help/2021/05.

Gonchar, Michael. "10 Intriguing Photographs to Teach Close Reading and Visual Thinking Skills." The Learning Network. Accessed March 8, 2022. learning.blogs.nytimes.com/2015/02/27/10-intriguing-photographs-to-teach-close-reading-and-visual-thinking-skills/.

Hattie, John, et al. "Feedback That Leads to Improvement in Student Essays: Testing the Hypothesis That 'Where to Next' Feedback Is Most Powerful." *Frontiers in Education* 6 (2021), doi.org/10.3389/feduc.2021.645758.

Hattie, John, and Helen Timperley. "The Power of Feedback." *Review of Educational Research* 77, no. 1 (March 2007): 81–112.

Hattie, John, Jill Crivelli, Kristin Van Gompel, Patti West-Smith, and Kathryn Wike. "Feedback That Leads to Improvement in Student Essays: Testing the Hypothesis That 'Where to Next' Feedback Is Most Powerful." *Frontiers in Education* 6 (2021). doi.org/10.3389/feduc.2021.645758.

Heid, Markham. "Are Audiobooks as Good for You as Reading? Here's What Experts Say." *Time*. September 6, 2018. time.com/5388681/audiobooks-reading-books/.

Henderson, M., and M. Phillips. "Video-Based Feedback on Student Assessment: Scarily Personal." *Australasian Journal of Educational Technology* 31, no. 1.

Herrmann, Zachary. "6 Ways to Guide Students to More Authentic Work in PBL." October 27, 2021. edutopia.org/article/6-ways-guide-students-more-authentic-work-pbl.

Howe, Christine, and Manzoorul Abedin. "Classroom Dialogue: A Systematic Review across Four Decades of Research." *Cambridge Journal of Education* 43, no. 3 (September 2013): 325–56.

Hussein, Bassam. "Addressing Collaboration Challenges in Project-Based Learning: The Student's Perspective." *Education Sciences* 11, article 434.

Indrisano, Roselmina, and Jeanne S. Chall. "Literacy Development." *Journal of Education* 177, no. 1 (January 1995): 63–83.

Krashen, S. D. "Free Voluntary Reading: Still a Very Good Idea." In *Explorations in Language Acquisition and Use*, by S. D. Krashen, 15–29. Portsmouth, NH: Heinemann, 2003.

Literacy Design Collaborative. "LDC." LDC Template Task Collection 2.0. 2013. ccsoh.us/cms/lib/OH01913306/Centricity/Domain/207/Rubrics%20LDC%202.0.pdf.

McAllum, Ruth. "Reciprocal Teaching: Critical Reflection on Practice." *Kairaranga* 15, no. 1 (2014): 26–35.

Meyer, Anne, David Gordon, and David H. Rose. *Universal Design for Learning: Theory and Practice*. Wakefield, MA: CAST Professional Publishing, 2015.

Minero, Emelina. "4 Steps of Student Self-Assessment." George Lucas Educational Foundation. October 4, 2016. edutopia.org/practice/mastering-self-assessment-deepening-independent-learning-through-arts.

Mitchell, John, and Lynne Rogers. "Staff Perceptions of Implementing Project-Based Learning in Engineering Education." *European Journal of English Education* 45: 349–62.

Montgomery, Joel R. "Using Audio Books to Improve Reading and Academic Performance." Working paper. 2009. files.eric.ed.gov/fulltext/ED505947.pdf.

Montroy, Janelle J., et al. "The Development of Self-Regulation across Early Childhood." *Developmental Psychology* 52, no. 11 (November 2016): 1744–62.

National Center for Education Statistics. "Undergraduate Retention and Graduation Rates." May 2021. nces.ed.gov/programs/coe/indicator/ctr.

Nguyen, Hoa P. "How to Use Interleaving to Foster Deeper Learning." George Lucas Educational Foundation. June 11, 2021. edutopia.org/article/how-use-interleaving-foster-deeper-learning.

Ninomiya, Shuichi. "The Possibilities and Limitations of Assessment for Learning: Exploring the Theory of Formative Assessment and the notion of 'Closing the Learning Gap.'" *Educational Studies in Japan: International Yearbook* 79, no. 10: 79–91.

Novak, Katie, and Lainie Rowell. "A Simple Way for Educators to Get the Feedback They Need." *Inspired Ideas.* November 22, 2021. medium.com/inspired-ideas-prek-12/a-simple-way-for-educators-to-get-the-feedback-they-need-559e9c6bc60.

Olmstead, Christine. "Using Technology to Increase Parent Involvement in Schools." *TechTrends* 57, no. 6 (October 18, 2013): 28–37.

Parrish, Nina. "How to Teach Self-Regulation." George Lucas Educational Foundation. August 22, 2018. edutopia.org/article/how-teach-self-regulation.

Posey, Allison, and Katie Novak. *Unlearning: Changing Your Beliefs and Your Classroom with UDL*. Wakefield, MA: CAST Professional Publishing, 2020.

Project Zero. "PZ's Thinking Routines Toolbox." Harvard University Graduate School of Education. Accessed March 5, 2022. pz.harvard.edu/thinking-routines.

Ryan, R., and E. Deci. "Intrinsic and Extrinsic Motivation from a Self-Determination Theory Perspective: Definitions, Theory, Practices, and Future Directions." *Contemporary Educational Psychology* 61, doi.org/10.1016/j.cedpsych.2020.101860.

Said, Khalid, and Abdelouahid El Mouzrati. "Investigating Teacher Written Corrective Feedback as a Formative Assessment Tool." *Arab World English Journal* 9, no. 4: 232–41.

Santa, Carol Minnick, Lynn T. Havens, and Bonnie J. Valdes. *Project CRISS: Creating Independence Through Student-Owned Strategies*. Dubuque, IA: Kendall Hunt, 2004.

Setyaningrum, Wahyu. "Blended Learning: Does It Help Students in Understanding Mathematical Concepts?" *Jurnal Riset Pendidikan Matematika* 5, no. 2 (November 22, 2018): 244–53.

Siegesmund, Amy. "Increasing Student Metacognition and Learning through Classroom-Based Learning Communities and Self-Assessment." *Journal of Microbiology & Biology Education* 17, no. 2 (May 2016): 204–14.

Siegesmund, Amy. "Using Self-Assessment to Develop Metacognition and Self-Regulated Learners." *FEMS Microbiology Letters* 364, no. 11. doi.org/10.1093/femsle/fnx096.

Spencer, John. "What Happens When Students Launch Their Work to an Audience?" November 20, 2020. spencerauthor.com/launch-virtual/.

Staples, Kelli E., and Jennifer A. Diliberto. "Guidelines for Successful Parent Involvement: Working with Parents of Students with Disabilities." *Teaching Exceptional Children* 42, no. 6.

Stover, Sheri, Sharon Heilmann, and Amelia Hubbard. "Learner-Centered Design: Is Sage on the Stage Obsolete?" *Journal of Effective Teaching in Higher Education* 1, no. 1 (November 3, 2018): 3.

Swan, Karen. "Social Construction of Knowledge and the Community of Inquiry Framework." In *Open and Distance Education Theory Revisited: Implications for the Digital Era*, edited by Insung Jung, 57–65. Singapore: Springer, 2019.

Tan, Richard K., Ronald Polong, Leila Collates, and Joel Torres. "Influence of Small Group Discussion on the English Oral Communication Self-Efficacy of Filipino ESL Learners in Central Luzon." *TESOL International Journal* 15, no . 1 (2020): 100–106.

Top Non-Profits. "Know Your Target Audience: 10 Questions to Ask." 2021. topnonprofits.com/know-your-target-audience-10-questions-to-ask/.

Voelkel, S., and L. V. Mello. "Audio Feedback—Better Feedback?" *Bioscience Education* 22, no. 1: 16–30.

Vygotsky, L. S. *Mind in Society: The Development of Higher Psychological Processes*. Cambridge, MA: Harvard University Press, 1980.

Wiggins, Grant. "EJ in Focus: Real-World Writing: Making Purpose and Audience Matter." *English Journal* 98, no. 5 (2009): 29–37.

Yurdakal, Ibrahim Halil. "Investigation of the 4th Grade Primary School Students' Attitudes towards Reading in the Scope of Different Variables." *World Journal of Education* 9, no. 3 (June 25, 2019): 46.

ACKNOWLEDGMENTS

Cat

Katie—I am so grateful George and AJ introduced us! I knew from the moment we met on that first Zoom call that I wanted to work with and learn from you. You are dynamic, kind, intelligent, and full of sparkle! Our collaborations have made me a better writer and more thoughtful educator. Thank you for saying "yes" that morning when I pitched this book idea! It would not be the book it is without your insights and expertise. I cannot wait to spend a week with you in Panama, cooking up our next writing adventure!

Christopher—When I had the idea for this book, I could not wait to tell you all about it. I knew you'd be thrilled and want to hear every detail. Thank you for listening when I need to think out loud, making yummy breakfasts, bringing me endless cups of coffee, leaving ridiculous Post-It notes all over the house, and reminding me to downshift when I need a break. Having a partner who makes me feel seen, heard, and supported is a gift. I love you.

George, I'm so grateful for your professional matchmaking and for your belief in our work.

Thank you Paige, Sal, and Ashley for all you've done to make this book happen!

Katie

Cat—Goodness gracious, do I love working with you! I am so blessed to have such strong, brilliant, beautiful women in my life. You are a huge part of that circle and you inspire and push me to continue to write, present, teach, and learn every day. I am so excited about our trip to Panama and can't wait until we can pull off the winter writing retreat in some tropical remote location. Love you, lady.

To George. I am so thankful to you for so many reasons. Thank you for being an amazing friend, supporter, colleague, and publisher. And thank you to you and AJ for setting me up with Cat. I love a good ole blind professional date and clearly, we hit it off. Can't wait until we run our marathon. Hell, let's make it an ultra. The sky is the limit.

To the team that helped bring this book to life—Paige, Sal, and Ashley. Thank you.

Ash—I will never tell you to "Shine brighter elsewhere."

To Lon. For all the coffees, laughs, and love. You are everything. Well, except funny. That's me.

And to my babies. Boden, Brec, Aylin, and Torin (see, I went in reverse order this time!). Each of you is my favorite child. I promise. Xoxoxo Momma

ABOUT THE AUTHORS

Catlin Tucker

Dr. Catlin Tucker is an author, international trainer, and keynote speaker. She was named Teacher of the Year in 2010 in Sonoma County, where she taught for sixteen years. Catlin earned her BA in English from the University of California at Los Angeles, her single subject teaching credential and masters in education from the University of California at Santa Barbara, and her doctorate in learning technologies from Pepperdine University. Currently, Catlin is working as a blended learning coach, education consultant, and professor in the masters of arts in teaching program at Pepperdine University.

Catlin works with schools and districts all over the world supporting their transition to blended learning. Catlin designs and facilitates professional learning to help leaders, coaches, and teachers to cultivate the mindset, skill set, and tool set necessary to thrive in blended learning environments. Catlin encourages educators to blend the best aspects of technology and tradition to shift students to the center of learning. She also works with leadership teams and instructional coaches to explore how they can support this shift by developing a robust professional learning infrastructure that weaves professional learning into the fabric of the school.

Catlin has written a series of best-selling books on blended learning, which include *UDL and Blended Learning, Balance With Blended Learning, Blended Learning In Action*, and *Power Up Blended Learning*. She is active on Twitter @Catlin_Tucker and writes an internationally ranked blog at CatlinTucker.com.

Katie Novak

Katie Novak, EdD, is an internationally renowned education consultant, author, graduate instructor at the University of Pennsylvania, and former assistant superintendent of schools. With twenty years of experience in teaching and administration, an earned doctorate in curriculum and teaching, and ten published books, Katie designs and presents workshops both nationally and internationally, focusing on the implementation of inclusive practices, Universal Design for Learning (UDL), multitiered systems of support, and universally designed leadership. Her work has impacted educators worldwide as her contributions and collaborations have built upon the foundation for an educational framework that is critical for student success.

Dr. Novak is the author of the best-selling books *UDL Now! A Teacher's Guide to Applying Universal Design for Learning in Today's*

Classrooms; *Innovate inside the Box*, with George Couros; *Equity by Design*, with Mirko Chardin; and *UDL and Blended Learning*, with Catlin Tucker.

Dr. Novak's work has been highlighted in many publications including *Edutopia*, *Cult of Pedagogy*, *Language* magazine, *NAESP Principal*, *ADDitude* magazine, *Huffington Post*, *Principal Leadership*, *District Administrator*, *ASCD Education Update*, and *School Administrator*. She is active on Twitter @KatieNovakUDL. You can also connect with her at novakeducation.com.

More from

IMPRESS

ImpressBooks.org

Empower
What Happens when Students Own Their Learning
by A.J. Juliani and John Spencer

Learner-Centered Innovation
Spark Curiosity, Ignite Passion, and Unleash Genius
by Katie Martin

Unleash Talent
Bringing Out the Best in Yourself and the Learners You Serve
by Kara Knollmeyer

Reclaiming Our Calling
Hold On to the Heart, Mind, and Hope of Education
by Brad Gustafson

Take the L.E.A.P.
Ignite a Culture of Innovation
by Elisabeth Bostwick

Drawn to Teach
An Illustrated Guide to Transforming Your Teaching
written by Josh Stumpenhorst and illustrated by Trevor Guthke

Math Recess
Playful Learning in an Age of Disruption
by Sunil Singh and Dr. Christopher Brownell

Innovate inside the Box
Empowering Learners Through UDL and Innovator's Mindset
by George Couros and Katie Novak

Personal & Authentic
Designing Learning Experiences That Last a Lifetime
by Thomas C. Murray

Learner-Centered Leadership
A Blueprint for Transformational Change in Learning Communities
by Devin Vodicka

Kids These Days
A Game Plan for (Re)Connecting with Those We Teach, Lead, & Love
by Dr. Jody Carrington

UDL and Blended Learning
Thriving in Flexible Learning Landscapes
by Katie Novak and Catlin Tucker

Teachers These Days
Stories & Strategies for Reconnection
by Dr. Jody Carrington and Laurie McIntosh

Because of a Teacher
Stories of the Past to Inspire the Future of Education
written and curated by George Couros

Because of a Teacher, Volume 2
Stories from the First Years of Teaching
written and curated by George Couros

Evolving Education
Shifting to a Learner-Centered Paradigm
by Katie Martin

Adaptable
How to Create an Adaptable Curriculum and Flexible Learning Experiences That Work in Any Environment
by A.J. Juliani

Lead from Where You Are
Building Intention, Connection, and Direction in Our Schools
by Joe Sanfelippo

Evolving with Gratitude
Small Practices in Learning Communities That Make a Big Difference with Kids, Peers, and the World
by Lainie Rowell

Learning in the Zone
The 7 Habits of Meta-Learners
by Sonny Magana

CPSIA information can be obtained
at www.ICGtesting.com
Printed in the USA
LVHW051247050323
740982LV00003B/755